Frank Zöllner

Leonardo da Vinci

1452–1519

The Complete Paintings

TASCHEN

KÖLN LONDON LOS ANGELES MADRID PARIS TOKYO

Contents

LEONARDO DA VINCI — LIFE AND WORK
Frank Zöllner

Indeed, the great Leonardo remained like a child for the whole of his life in more than one way; it is said that all great men are bound to retain some infantile part. Even as an adult he continued to play, and this was another reason why he often appeared uncanny and incomprehensible to his contemporaries.

SIGMUND FREUD, 1910

I The young artist in Florence 1469–1480

Amongst the great figures of the Italian Renaissance, Leonardo da Vinci remains one of the most enigmatic of them all. Although he has bequeathed to us the most extensive body of writings of any artist of his generation, rarely amongst these thousands of pages of manuscript do we find references to his personal opinions and feelings. We do not even have a very clear idea of what he looked like, and tend to picture him in two ways. On the one hand, we imagine Leonardo as a bearded old man – as he has come down to us in the so-called Turin *Self-portrait* (ill. p. 10) and in a drawing by his pupil, Francesco Melzi (1493–1570; ill. p. 8). On the other hand, we see him as a handsome youth, the embodiment of the Florentine Early Renaissance ideal of beauty, of the type that Leonardo himself drew many times and which adorns, in an androgynous variation, the signet of an "Achademia Leonardi Vinci" which he founded (ill. p. 8). Rarely, in visualizing Leonardo's appearance, do we imagine a man in his prime, an artist between the ages of 30 and 60, the period of his career during which he produced most of his works. The reasons for this are essentially twofold: in the figure of the old man with the flowing beard, Leonardo appears to us as the wise inquirer and thinker, as someone who, through long years of study, has acquired a wealth of "scientific" knowledge and reached a venerable old age in the meantime. In the handsome youth, on the other hand, we see the untutored genius who has outstripped his old teacher even before completing his apprenticeship (see below).

The wisdom associated with old age is thus just as much a characteristic of Leonardo and his art as the precocious talent that was with him from his earliest youth and would remain with him to his life's end. In his *Lives of the Artists*, first published in 1550, the biographer Giorgio Vasari (1511–1574) takes up the story of the talented young Leonardo, who was born on 15 April 1452 in Vinci, not far from Florence. In his typically anecdotal fashion, Vasari describes how Leonardo's artistic career began as follows: Ser Piero, Leonardo's father, "one day took some of Leonardo's drawings along to Andrea del Verrocchio

(who was a close friend of his) and earnestly begged him to say whether it would be profitable for the boy to study design. Andrea was amazed to see what extraordinary beginnings Leonardo had made and he urged Piero to make him study the subject. So Piero arranged for Leonardo to enter Andrea's workshop. The boy was delighted with this decision, and he began to practise not only one branch of the arts but all the branches in which design plays a part."

While the tale of the young genius who had already mastered the fundamentals of his future métier even before commencing his apprenticeship may be a commonplace of art history, it undoubtedly contains a grain of truth. For the young Leonardo must have demonstrated an extraordinary aptitude for drawing at a very early age. No other artist of his generation left behind such an extensive, authentic and at the same time innovative graphic œuvre. Leonardo's earliest surviving drawings from the 1470s already display the talented handling of metalpoint and pen to which Vasari pays enthusiastic tribute. Typical of Leonardo's sheer pleasure in drawing are the small, often playful sketches of figures in motion, executed with short, energetic strokes of the pen. Exercises in rendering three-dimensional objects are thereby joined by excursions into pure imagination. At the same time, other drawings from Leonardo's early years demonstrate the scrupulous accuracy and graphic precision that all artists had to learn during their training.

One such is his silverpoint drawing of an older man, the so-called *Antique Warrior* (ill. p. 9), probably executed *c.* 1472 or shortly afterwards, in which Leonardo takes up a figural type employed in his master Verrocchio's (1435–1488) workshop and derived from the works of classical antiquity. It is possible that young artists such as Leonardo honed their draughtsman's skills by making studies of works of this kind. Indeed, at one point in his posthumously compiled *Trattato di pittura* (*Treatise on Painting*), Leonardo advises artists to copy the works of "good masters" in order to learn how to "represent objects well in re-

lief" (McM 63). Whatever the case, we may assume that the young Leonardo, like other artists at the start of their career, trained his hand and eye by making studies of older works of art, and in particular, too, of nature.

Typical of such studies of nature are the sketches that Leonardo produced during his apprenticeship, including his earliest dated drawing, today housed in the Uffizi in Florence (ill. p. 11). In the top left-hand corner, in his own characteristic mirror-writing, are the words "on the day of St Mary of the Snow Miracle 5 August 1473". Executed in pen and ink over a barely visible preparatory sketch, the study shows a view of a valley bordered by hills, leading away towards a distant horizon. The drawing is thought to portray a real landscape, but opinions vary widely as to the identity of the fortified hilltop village on the left. Leonardo's drawing not only bears witness to the increasing importance of studies from nature in the 15th century, but also demonstrates the efforts artists were making to subordinate the features of the visible world to their own creative will. Thus, for instance, the crowns of the individual trees on the hill on the right are simply sketched in with rapid hatching. In places these hatchings combine to form oscillating patterns that go well beyond the immediate imitation of nature. It is also possible, however, that this same sketch – generally considered one of the earliest autonomous landscape studies in art history – takes up elements used by Leonardo's teacher, Verrocchio. Patterns and sections of landscape similar to those in Leonardo's drawing can in fact be found in the backgrounds of several of Verrocchio's Madonna paintings, as can the motif of vegetation growing over the edge of a cliff. The younger artist perhaps oriented himself in his drawings – as later in his smaller paintings (see below) – towards the style of his teacher.

A typical product of Verrocchio's workshop is the small *Dreyfus Madonna*, which is occasionally attributed to Leonardo himself (Cat. II/ill. p. 12) and which reveals some parallels with Leonardo's *Madonna of the Carnation* (Cat. III/ill. p. 13). This little panel, which is also known as the *Madonna of the Pomegranate*, derives from a compositional type found chiefly in Venice. Verrocchio probably encountered this type during a trip to Venice in 1469 and subsequently introduced it to Florence. In her left hand, the very youthful-looking Virgin holds a split, ripe pomegranate, a symbol of Christ's Passion. The infant Jesus has taken a seed of the pomegranate with his right hand and holds it up to his mother with an inquiring gaze. This symbolic reference to Christ's future Passion is reinforced by the stone parapet running across the foreground, which can be interpreted as a reference to the altar and thus to the Eucharistic Sacrifice of Christ. This symbolism is even clearer in other variations on the same compositional theme issuing from the workshops of Verrocchio and Giovanni Bellini (c. 1433–c. 1516), in which roses and cherries rest on top of the parapet as symbols of the Eucharist. In the context of such contemplative paintings, the parapet thus links the elements making up the intimate devotional scene with a reminder of Christ's Passion.

That the *Dreyfus Madonna* was intended as the object of quiet prayer in a private home is further underlined by the striking contrast within the picture between interior and exterior. The Virgin and Child are seated in a positively gloomy room. A short stretch of wall behind the Virgin's head gives way to two windows, one on either side, which are bounded in turn by grey pilasters and further sections of wall. This narrow interior is contrasted with the view, through the windows behind, out onto a bright and expansive landscape, which the artist has portrayed with some care. This landscape reveals parallels with Flemish and Umbrian works from the years around 1470, for example in the highlights placed on the trees in the middle ground and in the overall layout of the scenery. The Virgin's blue mantle, on the other hand, is more typical of Tuscan – and specifically Florentine – painting: its folds spill over the parapet like an altar cloth and recall similar draperies in the paintings of Lorenzo di Credi (c. 1458–1537).

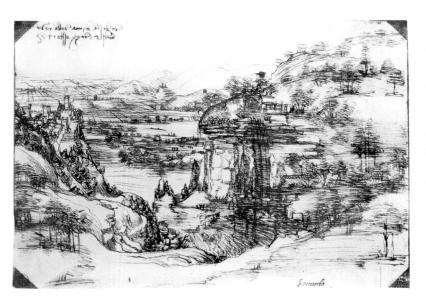

Page 10:
Leonardo (?)
Head of a Bearded Man (so-called Self-portrait),
c. 1510–1515 (?)
Red chalk, 333 x 215 mm
Turin, Biblioteca Reale, Inv. 15571

Arno Landscape, 5 August 1473
Pen and ink, 190 x 285 mm
Florence, Galleria degli Uffizi, Gabinetto dei Disegni e delle Stampe, Inv. 436E

It was one of those faces that seem to belong more to the imaginary realm of poetry than to the raw reality of life: contours that recall da Vinci, the noble oval with naïve dimples and sentimentally pointed chin of the Lombard School.

HEINRICH HEINE, 1837

The *Dreyfus Madonna* is in many respects characteristic of small-format devotional panels of the second half of the 15th century. Behind the tiny piece of pomegranate, barely visible in the Infant's right hand, lies the artistic assumption that the viewer is standing very close to the painting and thus that the panel itself is hanging in a domestic setting. Indeed, Verrocchio's *Dreyfus Madonna* seems to echo the recommendations of Fra Giovanni Dominici (*c.* 1356–1419), a Dominican preacher who in his *Regola del governo di cura famigliare* of 1403 set out, in great detail, the beneficial effects of having small devotional paintings in the family home. Pictures of holy infants should be hung in the house, he advised, since these would appeal to children from a very tender age. Children would be drawn to such pictures, would see themselves in the infants portrayed and model themselves upon them. Pictures of the Virgin Mary with the infant Jesus in her arms were also to be recommended, with Jesus holding a bird or a pomegranate in his little hands; equally praiseworthy were portrayals of the infant Jesus asleep or standing in front of his mother. Dominici thus assigned a specific didactic function to such devotional panels, with whose subjects younger viewers, in particular, could identify.

Leonardo's *Madonna of the Carnation* (Cat. III/ill. p. 13) was probably conceived with a similar function in mind. This is possibly the painting to which Vasari is referring when he describes, in his *Life of Leonardo*, "a Madonna, a very fine work which came into the possession of Pope Clement VII (reg. 1523–1534); one of the details in this picture was a vase of water containing some flowers, painted with wonderful realism, which had on them dewdrops that looked more convincing than the real thing." Probably executed while Leonardo was still with Verrocchio, the panel takes up elements of Early Netherlandish painting in its slender pillars in the middle ground and its background landscape. The figures of the Virgin and the infant Jesus, on the other hand, clearly draw on the pictorial forms employed in Verrocchio's workshop. As was the convention in devotional panels of this kind, Leonardo's portrayal of the loving relationship between Mary and the infant Jesus is complemented with a number of familiar Christian symbols. The Holy Child is reaching out, in the still clumsy manner of a young infant, for a red carnation, a symbol of the Passion of Christ, which thus introduces into this scene of childlike innocence a reference to the later Crucifixion awaiting the Saviour. Equally symbolic in its intention is the crystal vase filled with flowers in the bottom right-hand corner, a clear reference to the purity and virginity of Mary. On another level, meanwhile, motifs such as the carnation and the crystal vase, which demand great skill on the part of the artist, allowed Leonardo to give an impressive demonstration of his talent – a talent also exhibited in the masterly swathe of drapery bunched in the Virgin's lap, whose intense hue gives life to the dark foreground and corresponds in compositional terms with the brightness of the Virgin's face and neck. In contrast to comparable works by Verrocchio, Leonardo also brings mother and child closer together and thereby arrives, albeit still imperfectly, at the pyramidal composition that would later become the hallmark of High Renaissance painting. The *Madonna of the Carnation* also differs from the majority of the paintings issuing from Verrocchio's workshop in its painting technique. By using oil as his binding medium, Leonardo was able to achieve softer transitions between the individual areas of colour. It is this, for example, that lends the background the evocative atmosphere lacking in Verrocchio's landscapes, for all their profusion of vegetation, and which would characterize later paintings such as the *Mona Lisa* and the *Virgin and Child with St Anne*.

A difference in technique between master and pupil also emerges in *The Baptism of Christ* (Cat. IV/ill. p. 17). This large altarpiece, which was probably originally destined for the Vallombrose church of San Salvi just outside Florence, was begun by Verrocchio some time around 1470–1472. Parts of the background landscape, however, were completed by Leonardo around 1475 or soon afterwards.

Workshop of Andrea del Verrocchio (?)
Madonna of the Pomegranate (Dreyfus Madonna), *c.* 1470–1472 (?) or later
*Tempera and oil (?) on oak, 15.7 x 12.8 cm
Washington, DC, National Gallery of Art, Samuel H. Kress Collection, Inv. 1144 (K1850)*

Andrea del Verrocchio (?) and Workshop
Virgin and Child, *c.* 1475 (?)
*Tempera on wood, 74 x 46 cm
Berlin, Staatliche Museen zu Berlin – Preussischer Kulturbesitz, Gemäldegalerie*

Page 13:
Madonna of the Carnation (Madonna with a Vase of Flowers), *c.* 1472–1478 (?)
*Tempera (?) and oil on poplar (?), 62.3 x 48.5 cm
Munich, Bayerische Staatsgemäldesammlungen, Alte Pinakothek, Inv. 7779 (1493)*

The angel kneeling on the far left, his face turned towards the central scene, is also the work of the young Leonardo. As Vasari tells us, "at that time Verrocchio was working on a panel picture showing the Baptism of Christ by St John, for which Leonardo painted an angel who was holding some garments; and despite his youth, he executed it in such a manner that his angel was far better than the figures painted by Andrea. This was the reason why Andrea would never touch colours again, he was so ashamed that a boy understood their use better than he did." Vasari, who was born as late as 1511, is known for supplementing the gaps in his knowledge about earlier art history with entertaining anecdotes, and the tale about Leonardo working on Andrea del Verrocchio's *Baptism of Christ* sounds like a prime example. However, modern-day technical analysis of the panel has fully confirmed the information provided by the biographer from Aretino. Even his bold assertion that Verrocchio abandoned painting after seeing what his extraordinarily gifted pupil could do may not be a piece of pure fiction. It is a fact that scarcely any paintings can be attributed to Verrocchio after the completion of the *Baptism of Christ* – a point that may also have struck Vasari.

Already employing a distinct and innovative technique, Leonardo's angel in Verrocchio's painting also adopts a pose infused with a typically Leonardesque sense of movement. Thus his upper body faces one way while his head turns to look in the other direction, and the movement of his left elbow is taken up again in the position of his right upper arm. The angel is distinguished, too, by the softness of his face, its gentle modelling distinctly different from the harder skin tones usually found in Verrocchio's work (ill. pp. 18/19). The same applies to the figure of Christ in the centre of the painting, which – close inspections have revealed – was reworked in oils at a later stage. Here, too, the flesh of Christ's body appears softer than that of John the Baptist, painted by Verrocchio in the original tempera.

In another significant contribution to Verrocchio's panel, and one that looks forward to his own later works, Leonardo also repainted the left-hand background in oils. What had started out as a view of shrubs and trees now became a very different landscape of water and rocky cliffs. In executing this new background, Leonardo created a sense of depth typical of his art: the landscape stretches away in a seemingly natural manner right into the far distance. Limpid waters play around precipitous cliffs; a warm light falls more or less evenly from the left across the group of figures in the foreground; dramatically cleft mountains contrast with the smooth, horizontal expanse of water and fade in the distance into a soft blur; directly above the horizon, the blue of the sky lightens until it becomes a gleaming white. Similar horizons, and a

certain predilection for rocky landscapes, can be found in Leonardo's later works, where their atmospheric effects are exploited even more fully.

The overall composition and iconographical details of Verrocchio and Leonardo's panel are based both on the descriptions of the Baptism of Christ in the Gospels (Matthew 3:3–17; Mark 1:9–11; John 1:26–36) and on earlier pictorial conventions: Christ, who has removed most of his clothes, is standing on the rocky bed of the river Jordan and is being baptized by John, stepping forwards from the right. Above him hovers the dove of the Holy Spirit, above which in turn we can see the hands of God the Father. The presence of the dove has caused the bird of prey on the right to take flight: a symbolic adversary of the Holy Spirit, it is here fleeing the Holy Spirit's greater power.

On the left-hand side of the picture, the angel painted by Leonardo is holding Christ's robe, its original colour now somewhat faded. Some have sought to identify this figure with Archangel Michael, who was particularly venerated by the Vallombrose monks of San Salvi, for whom the altarpiece was probably painted. Behind the angel, a palm tree provides a formal conclusion to the foreground scene. This palm tree – lent a somewhat archaic character by its schematic portrayal – represents the Tree of Paradise, symbolizing salvation and life, and also pointing to Christ's future triumph over death. A similar iconography underlies the staff in John's left hand, too, whose banderole bears the words ECCE AGNIVS D[ei, ecce qui tollit peccatum mundi] (John 1:29; "Behold the Lamb of God, who takes away the sin of the world"). These words are a reference both to Christ's sacrifice on the cross and to the panel's intended function as an altarpiece: they are reminder of the Sacrifice of Christ being re-enacted in the celebration of Mass at the altar, directly in front of the altarpiece portraying the Baptism of Christ.

Although, in his use of oils in the *Baptism of Christ*, Leonardo demonstrates a certain degree of technical independence, he was still working in Verrocchio's workshop during this period. It is not surprising, therefore, that almost all of Leonardo's early paintings reveal formal parallels with the works of his master and start from the same compositional premises. One such is the *Annunciation*, which was largely executed by Leonardo and today hangs in the Uffizi in Florence (Cat. V/ill. pp. 20/21). The decorative sarcophagus placed before Mary, for instance, corresponds closely, in its rich ornamentation, with a similar sarcophagus that Andrea del Verrocchio sculpted in 1472 for the Old Sacristy in San Lorenzo in Florence. This also provides us with a provisional point of reference for the dating of the *Annunciation*, which remains the subject of much debate.

As a youth, the enigmatic Leonardo is supposed to have said to his maths tutor: "He is a poor pupil who does not surpass his master."

OSKAR KOKOSCHKA, 1951

Andrea del Verrocchio and Leonardo
The Baptism of Christ,
c. 1470–1472 and c. 1475
Oil and tempera on poplar,
180 x 151.3 cm
Florence, Galleria degli Uffizi,
Inv. 8358

Annunciation, *c.* **1473–1475 (?)**
Oil and tempera on poplar,
100 x 221.5 cm
Florence, Galleria degli Uffizi,
Inv. 1618

It is true that decorum should be observed, that is, movements should announce the motion of the mind of the one who is moving. Accordingly, if the painter has to represent someone who must show fearful reverence, the figure should not be done with such audacity and presumption that the effect seems to be despair, or the uttering of a command.

LEONARDO DA VINCI, MK 521

The attribution of the painting is similarly a matter of some controversy, although a study by Leonardo for the right sleeve of the Archangel Gabriel is considered an indication that he was responsible for a considerable part of the composition. The painting, it may also be said, does not give the impression of being the work of a fully independent and mature artist such as Verrocchio. In comparison to the *Baptism of Christ*, for example, the *Annunciation* reveals a greater number of *pentimenti* – places where the overall composition and individual details differ in the final version from the original design. These suggest that the painting was executed by an artist still lacking in compositional experience, like Leonardo. Fingerprints on the panel are a further indication that the young Leonardo was here at work: dabbing his freshly applied oil paints with his fingers and the ball of his right hand was one of Leonardo's particular trademarks in Florence.

The time and place of the Annunciation are clearly laid down: we are in Nazareth, where on 25 March the Archangel Gabriel appears to Mary in the garden, interrupts her reading the Bible (Isaiah 7:14), and informs her that she has been chosen to bear the Son of God (Protevangelium of James 11; Luke 1:26–38). The present scene, which largely follows 15th-century conventions, is flanked to the right by relatively contemporary architecture. The middle ground is concluded by a low wall rising to about knee-height and interrupted half way along by a small gap. Through this gap – which also serves to frame the gesture of greeting by Gabriel and the lily in his left hand – we can see a path leading away into the distance. Concluding the composition are a number of trees, sharply silhouetted against the bright sky, and beyond them mountains. A number of details within the painting carry a deep-

er meaning. Thus the white lily in Gabriel's hand is a symbol of Mary's purity, and the meadow in the foreground, with its many flowers, a reference to Nazareth, since according to *The Golden Legend* (1263/73) by Jacobus de Voragine (*c.* 1230–1298), Nazareth denotes "flower". There is significance, too, contained within the distant background, where in addition to the sea and the mountains we are also shown a port. This town by the sea is perhaps a reference to Marian symbolism: Mary was referred to in 15th-century liturgical books as *stella maris* (star of the sea) and as the sheltering harbour for all who had been shipwrecked on the sea of life (cf. Ch. III, IX). The maritime panorama in the background of the *Annunciation* may be inspired by just such ideas.

Annunciations, finally, fell into a number of subtly different categories. In the present painting, Gabriel's right hand forms what can be clearly identified as the traditional gesture of Annunciation, while Mary's left hand is raised in what at first sight appears a conventional gesture of greeting. Mary's particular gesture, however, may also signify that we are looking at a specific, *conturbatio* type of Annunciation. The *conturbatio* interpretation of the Annunciation focuses on Mary's disquiet at being suddenly confronted by an angel in her garden and being given the unusual news that she is to bear God's son. Leonardo's Mary, on the other hand, maintains considerably more composure than her terrified counterparts in other *conturbatio* Annunciations, such as those by Sandro Botticelli (1445–1510). To all appearances, in Leonardo's modification of the *conturbatio* motif we are already seeing the innovative treatment of a pictorial type. This is further confirmed by a look back at Verrocchio's *Baptism of Christ*, whose overall design remains much more heavily indebted to earlier treatments of the same

subject than does Leonardo's *Annunciation*. A similar conclusion emerges from a comparison of Leonardo's painting and a small *Annunciation* in the Louvre (Cat. VIII/ill. pp. 32/33), probably executed by Lorenzo di Credi, a fellow pupil in Verrocchio's workshop. Credi's composition adheres significantly more closely to established convention. The gestures made by his two figures, for example, are closely based on older paintings: while Gabriel raises his right hand, Mary folds her hands against her breast in the gesture of *humiliatio* (submission).

As already glimpsed in the *Baptism of Christ*, the background landscape in the Uffizi *Annunciation* looks forward to later paintings by Leonardo. It also demonstrates his masterly handling of the elements of water, air and light, which here bathe the steep foothills of the almost alpine ridges and peaks in the distance in an atmosphere of increasing density (ill. pp. 30/31). Leonardo would later describe similar phenomena in several places in his treatise on painting, for example when writing about the particular charm of horizons combining the elements of mountains and sea: "These horizons make a very fine sight in painting. It is true that there should be some mountains, behind one another, at the sides, with colour diminishing by degrees, as is required by the rule for the diminution of colours seen at great distances" (TPL 936). The atmospheric phenomena not described until 1508 in Leonardo's *Treatise on Painting* thus make their appearance considerably earlier in painting than in his theoretical writings. His artistic practice thus preceded his artistic theory.

Having worked and collaborated on larger paintings such as the *Annunciation* and the *Baptism of Christ*, Leonardo also continued, in the late 1470s, to paint small-format Madonnas. This emerges from a note of December 1478, in which Leonardo mentions that he is "starting the two Virgin Marys" ("incomincai le due Vergini Marie"), but is evidenced, too, by the numerous studies of the Virgin and the infant Jesus that he produced during this period (ill. p. 35). These sketches manifest the young artist's urge to test out – within the bounds of pictorial convention – the possibilities of movement and expression in a variety of subjects. At the same time, however, they also include experiments in pure flights of fancy, exercises in free artistic expression which are permissible in drawing but would be out of place in painting. Not all of Leonardo's extant drawings can therefore be taken as preliminary studies for actual paintings. A number of these drawings nevertheless lead at least indirectly to the so-called *Benois Madonna*, which may be seen as the finest of Leonardo's early interpretations of the Virgin and Child theme (Cat. VI/ill. p. 34).

The *Benois Madonna*, named after one of its former owners, stands out from similar works by other artists by virtue of its darker palette, its more pronounced contrasts of light and shade and its greater dynamism. Leonardo's preliminary studies for the composition themselves reveal a remarkable animation, but only in the final painting do the ideas spontaneously developed in the drawings fuse into a harmonious whole. The emotional bond between mother and child is given formal expression not just in their physical proximity, but even in their poses. Thus both figures adopt the same sitting position, with one leg bent and other extended, whereby the legs of the infant Jesus are a smaller, mirror-image version of those of his mother. In this the *Benois Madonna* anticipates Leonardo's *Virgin and Child with St Anne* (Cat.

XXVII/ill. p. 149), executed a few years later, in which the artist establishes a similar physical and at the same time genealogical relationship between the Virgin and her mother, St Anne. The fall of the draperies across the Virgin's right thigh in the *Benois Madonna* also appears to anticipate the later painting, and is even found in a related study from the period after 1510 (ill. p. 148).

In the *Benois Madonna*, which is dated on stylistic grounds to the years between 1475 and 1480, Leonardo makes his first appearance as an independent artist who has arrived at his own formal style. For in terms of its composition, technique and palette, the *Benois Madonna* differs profoundly from comparable products issuing from Verrocchio's workshop, and also from Leonardo's own earlier *Madonna of the Carnation*. Leonardo's growing independence is also evidenced by two documents dating from early 1478. In January of that year Leonardo was asked to paint a large altarpiece for the chapel of St Bernard in the Palazzo Vecchio, the Florentine seat of government. Leonardo's father, a successful notary who had built up a considerable reputation in Florence and had already done work for the Signoria (the city council), may have had a hand in securing this commission. But although Leonardo received a generous advance of 25 gold ducats in March, three months after the contract was signed, he probably never even started the painting. With the contract for the St Bernard chapel, nevertheless, Leonardo is legally documented for the first time as an independent artist.

A certain degree of independence is also demonstrated by Leonardo's *Portrait of Ginevra de' Benci* (Cat. VII/ill. p. 37) as regards its technique and its interpretation of the genre. This small portrait represents a first truly fixed point of reference in Leonardo's painted œuvre, since it is the earliest extant work that can be linked with two well-documented individuals: the sitter, Ginevra de' Benci (1457–c. 1520), a young woman very well known in Florence, and Bernardo Bembo (1433–1519), who probably commissioned the picture. The *Portrait of*

Ginevra de' Benci is Leonardo's first secular painting. Much more than his religious paintings, it succeeds in breaking away from the pictorial conventions of Verrocchio's workshop. The most striking feature of the portrait is the immediate proximity of the sitter both to the viewer and to the vegetation behind her; together they share virtually the entire pictorial plane. The young woman, Ginevra de' Benci, is brought right to the front of the picture. She is seated in front of a juniper bush, which seems to surround her head like a wreath and fills a large part of the background. Comparable "close-ups" were already to be found in Flemish portraits of the type introduced by Jan van Eyck (c. 1390–1441) a generation earlier, and subsequently popularized by Hans Memling (1435–1494; ill. p. 36) and Petrus Christus (c. 1410–1472/73). There are echoes of Flemish portraiture, too, in the format (the panel was originally longer, but was at some point trimmed along the bottom), in the naturalistic rendition of the juniper bush and in the sitter's pose. In contrast to her head, which faces almost frontally towards the viewer, Ginevra's upper body is angled almost diagonal to the pictorial plane, lending her – despite her rather listless expression – a certain dynamism. It is perhaps worth noting that Ginevra's genteel pallor was determined not by artistic considerations but by her sickly constitution, something expressly mentioned in a number of sources. The same sources also document Ginevra's aspirations as a poet and her admiration for Petrarch, interests which she shared with her platonic lover, Bernardo Bembo.

The juniper bush that, in conjunction with Ginevra's luminous face, dominates the portrait is more than a mere decorative accessory. Like a number of other plants, it was also a symbol of female virtue. Furthermore, the Italian word for juniper, *ginepro*, makes a play on the name of the sitter, Ginevra. More such allusions are explored on the reverse of the panel (Cat. VIIb/ill. p. 36), where a number of different plants are portrayed in meaningful combination: against a background painted to look like red porphyry marble, we see a branch of laurel, ju-

Pages 32/33:
Lorenzo di Credi, after
a design by Leonardo (?)
Annunciation, c. 1478 or 1485
Tempera on poplar, 16 x 60 cm
Paris, Musée du Louvre,
Inv. 1602A (1265)

Benois Madonna, c. 1478–1480
Oil on wood, transferred to canvas,
49.5 x 31 cm
St Petersburg, Hermitag

**Study for a Madonna with
a Cat, c. 1478–1480**
*Pen and ink over preliminary
stylus drawing, 132 x 95 mm*
London, British Museum,
Inv. 1856-6-21-1

**Studies of a Virgin and
Child (right, a study for
the Benois Madonna),
c. 1478–1480**
Pen and ink, 198 x 150 mm
London, British Museum,
Inv. 1860-6-16-100r

niper and palm, connected to each other by a scrolling banderole bearing, in capital letters, the words "VIRTVTEM FORMA DECORAT" – "Beauty Adorns Virtue". The inscription and the plant attributes thus underline the connection between virtue and beauty. In its imitation of red, durable and very rare porphyry marble, the reverse of the portrait speaks of the resilience of Ginevra's virtue. The laurel and palm branches that frame the scroll are associated with Bernardo Bembo, who commissioned the painting. His personal arms consisted of a laurel branch and a palm branch and, between them, the inscription "VIRTVS ET HONOR". The emblem on the reverse of the portrait, with its laurel, juniper and palm branches, therefore represents a cleverly adapted modification of Bembo's own motto: in exactly the same spot as the inscription that originally filled the space between the branches of laurel and palm, we now see a branch of juniper in allusion to Ginevra's name and virtue. The laurel and the palm also make reference to Ginevra's literary leanings, since in poetry inspired by Petrarch, their evergreen branches represented the ultimate expression of poetic aspiration. The palm frond is likewise another traditional symbol of virtue.

Lastly, the inscription "VIRTVTEM FORMA DECORAT", so closely intertwined with the plants symbolic of virtue, establishes a connection between beauty and virtue which, as well as being a theme of contemporary literature, is also found on the front of the panel, where Ginevra's physical beauty is to be understood as an expression of her virtue. The front and back of this portrait could thus hardly be connected more closely. On the front, the juniper bush frames Ginevra's beauty, while on the back the laurel, palm branch and inscription surround the juniper which represents the young woman portrayed on the front.

The importance of the *Portrait of Ginevra de' Benci* lies above all in the fact that Leonardo here broke away from the profile view traditionally employed in Florence for portraits of women. Such portraits often served as wedding gifts or as part of a bride's dowry and had to reflect a relatively rigid ideal of female behaviour, leaving virtually no room for dynamism in their composition. Ginevra de' Benci, by contrast, is portrayed by Leonardo not as a bride, but as the partner and literary equal of Bernardo Bembo. For this reason the artist portrays her in three-quarter view, something previously reserved primarily for portraits of men and granting the sitter greater personal presence in the picture. Not least as a result of this innovation, Leonardo succeeds in lending a psychological dimension to his sitter – something that would become the hallmark of Renaissance portraiture.

Undoubtedly crucial to this new development was Leonardo's interest in the possibilities of oil painting and his preference for dynamic figural composition, already apparent in his angel in *The Baptism of Christ* and in his drawings. The man who commissioned the portrait, Bernardo Bembo, may well also have had a part to play in the proceedings, however. He had earlier spent time as a Venetian envoy at the court of Charles the Bold in Burgundy, from where he returned with new expectations of portraiture, expectations that, in Florence, it required Leonardo to fulfil. The contact between Bembo and Leonardo, which was to prove decisive in the evolution of portraiture, may have been initiated via the Benci family. Ginevra's brother Giovanni (1456–1523) was a friend of Leonardo's, and when Giorgio Vasari came to write his *Lives*, Leonardo's unfinished *Adoration of the Magi* was still to be found in the house of Giovanni's son, Amerigo Benci. The importance of personal contacts of this kind for the genesis of works of art would be demonstrated by the commission for this same *Adoration* (cf. Ch. II).

Hans Memling
Portrait of a Young Man,
c. **1478–80 (?)**
Oil and tempera (?) on wood,
38 x 27 cm
Florence, Galleria degli Uffizi

Leonardo (?)
Portrait of Ginevra de' Benci
(reverse), *c.* **1478–1480**
Tempera (and oil?) on poplar,
38.8 x 36.7 cm
Washington, DC, National
Gallery of Art, Ailsa Mellon
Bruce Fund, 1967, Inv. 2326

Page 37:
**Portrait of Ginevra
de' Benci,** *c.* **1478–1480**
Oil and tempera on poplar,
38.8 x 36.7 cm
Washington, DC, National
Gallery of Art, Ailsa Mellon
Bruce Fund, 1967, Inv. 2326

Leonardo knows only the one, vast, eternal space, in which his figures float, so to speak. The one offers, within the pictorial framework, an ensemble of individual, contiguous objects, the other an extract from infinity.

OSWALD SPENGLER, 1917

II Professional breakthrough in Florence 1480–1482

With the commission for the chapel of St Bernard in the Palazzo Vecchio and through the *Portrait of Ginevra de'Benci*, Leonardo had for the first time had dealings with important patrons – on the one hand, with senior representatives of the Florentine government and, on the other, with the Benci family, who maintained commercial and social links with the most powerful family in the city, the Medici. Corresponding to his increased importance as an artist is the fact that Leonardo proceeded to execute his next two paintings, both of them large, outside Andrea del Verrocchio's workshop.

After completing the *Portrait of Ginevra de'Benci*, he embarked on a painting of *St Jerome*, today housed in the Vatican Museums (Cat. IX/ ill. p. 46). This picture, which suffered extensive damage in later years, remained unfinished, but still conveys an approximate idea of Leonardo's original intention. The saint is portrayed as a penitent in the wilderness, here indicated as a barren landscape dotted with small rocky outcrops. Wearing an expression of suffering, St Jerome is kneeling in almost the exact centre of the composition. His left hand touches the seam of his open robe while his right hand grasps a stone and is drawn back in preparation for a blow. On his emaciated, bony chest there is a dark patch in the region of his heart – in all likelihood a blood-soaked wound that the saint has inflicted on himself during his penance. At the lower edge of the painting lies a lion, Jerome's pet and attribute, whom the saint once helped by pulling a thorn out of his paw. Lying directly in front of St Jerome, the lion is watching the proceedings and, with his mouth wide open, seems to want to fuel the fervour with which Jerome is performing his penitential exercises (see below).

The saint himself is in fact – although this can be made out only with difficulty – looking towards a small crucifix rising parallel to the right-hand edge of the picture. He thereby establishes a link between his own suffering as a penitent and the Passion of Christ. In the right-hand background, in the saint's line of vision, is the façade of a Renaissance-style church – possibly a reference to the church of the Nativity in Bethlehem, as mentioned in *The Golden Legend*, where Jerome would spend his latter years and be buried.

In portraying St Jerome as an ascetic penitent, Leonardo follows a pictorial convention established earlier in the 15th century. He deviates from this tradition, however, in one important point: his Jerome has no beard. Furthermore, in comparison with other paintings of the same subject, Leonardo places much greater emphasis upon the barrenness of the rocky setting. His dramatic vision of St Jerome's penance and its location within a landscape devoid of vegetation were probably inspired directly or indirectly by a letter that Jerome wrote to Eustochium in the year 384, passages from which are cited in the entry on St Jerome in *The Golden Legend* and were made the subject of other depictions of the saint (cf. Bellini, ill. p. 47). In this moving letter – effectively an essay on the preservation of virginity formulated from the saint's ascetic viewpoint – Jerome argues for the renunciation of the pleasures of the flesh while at the same time describing the very real temptations to which, even in his capacity as a man of God, he too finds himself constantly exposed. There is nothing abstract about his appeals for virtue and his exhortations to asceticism, for in his letter Jerome also describes being tormented by the feeling of lust, a human failing that may have been equally familiar to the viewer. The corresponding passage of the letter runs as follows: "All the company I had was scorpions and wild beasts, yet at times I felt myself surrounded by clusters of pretty girls, and the fires of lust were lighted in my frozen body and moribund flesh. So it was that I wept continually and starved the rebellious flesh for weeks at a time. Often I joined day to night and did not stop beating my chest until the Lord restored my peace of mind."

Even if Leonardo's painting is unable to incorporate every last dramatic detail of Jerome's description, in its portrayal of the penitent saint it clearly conveys an emotional agony with which viewers

Page 45:
Detail of **Adoration of the Magi**, 1481/82
(ill. p. 49)

St Jerome, *c.* 1480–1482
Oil and tempera on walnut,
102.8 x 73.5 cm
Rome, Pinacoteca Vaticana,
Inv. 40337

Study of a Kneeling Angel,
c. 1480–1483
Pen and ink, 125 x 60 mm
London, British Museum,
Inv. 1913-6-17-1

Giovanni Bellini
St Jerome in the Dessert,
c. 1479
Tempera on wood, 151 x 113 cm
Florence, Galleria degli Uffizi

wracked by a similar inner conflict could identify. In a later passage of his letter, Jerome describes in more detail the solitary wilderness to which he banished himself, and how he deliberately increased his isolation by wandering ever further into its depths. "Angry and stern with myself, I plunged alone, deeper and deeper, into the wasteland. Wherever I saw a ravine, a rugged mountain or a jagged cliff, I knelt down to pray, I used them as a scourge for my sinful flesh." These rocks and cliffs are more than simply the characteristic features of a wilderness landscape, however. They also carry a symbolic meaning, one that Jerome reveals elsewhere in his letter: "It is impossible that man's innate ardour, arising from his depths, should leave his senses untouched. To him be praise and recognition, therefore, who kills sordid thoughts dead even as they are born and dashes them against the rocks. The rock, however, is Christ."

With its highly realistic portrayal of St Jerome in the act of penitence, the painting issues a strong statement to the viewer, who could meditate on the saint's ascetic and penitent pose in his prayers. The rocky landscape little more than outlined in the unfinished picture thereby becomes a metaphor for the faithful individual's constant battle against the temptations of the flesh, against "sordid" thoughts, as Jerome calls them. Lastly, the barrenness of the rocks – which is intended more than just metaphorically – is taken up in the ascetic, emaciated body of the saint.

Since Leonardo did not finish the painting, St Jerome probably never served its intended purpose as an altarpiece. The artist himself may have held on to it for a while, possibly right up to his death, after which it may have been sold to a collector. From the start of the 16th century, namely, and above all in the wake of Michelangelo (1475–1564), unfinished works of art began to be appreciated in their own right. Pictures were valued not simply for their religious content, but increasingly for such criteria as their inventiveness and artistic innovations. Here, from an early stage, lay one of Leonardo's strengths, for his art was based from the very beginning on "scientific" studies and ideas. In the suffering expression on the face of St Jerome, for example, he illustrates both his own and contemporary notions of physiognomy and physiology. The muscles and sinews of the saint's shoulder and neck may also be taken as an early indication of Leonardo's interest in the surface anatomy of the human body. His most detailed anatomical studies, which have come down to us in the so-called anatomical Manuscript A in the Royal Library at Windsor Castle, were not conducted until some time between c. 1508 and 1510, however. Leonardo's artistic interest in anatomy thus preceded his "scientific" exploration of the same field by many years.

What caused Leonardo to abandon work on St Jerome was probably the commission for an Adoration of the Magi (Cat. X/ill. p. 49) for the high altar of the Augustinian church of San Donato a Scopeto, just outside Florence. Leonardo's father, who administered the monastery's business affairs, may have been instrumental in setting up the commission in March 1481. The fact that a year later Leonardo left this painting unfinished, too, was probably due to his move to Milan. The commission was subsequently taken over by Filippino Lippi (1457–1504), whose own Adoration of the Magi was completed in 1496 (ill. p. 53). Another reason why Leonardo stopped work on the project may also have been the complex provisions of the contract, which contain a number of anomalies.

Dated July 1481, the corresponding document runs as follows: "Leonardo di Ser Piero da Vinci has undertaken as of March 1480 [i.e., 1481] to paint a panel for our main altarpiece which he is obliged to have completed in 24 or at the most 30 months. And in the event of his not bringing it to completion he will forfeit that part of it which he has done, and we shall be at liberty to do as we please with it. For painting this altarpiece he is to have one third of a holding in Valdelsa which was formerly the property of Simone, father of Brother Francesco, who bequeathed it with the following injunction, that when three years have elapsed from the time of its completion we may buy it back for 300 fiorini di sugello, and within this stipulated time he may not enter into any other undertaking about it. And he must supply his own colours, [and] gold, and meet any other expenses he might incur. And moreover he must pay from his own pocket the appropriate deposit into the Monte [delle Doti = a dowry fund] to provide a dowry to the value of 150 fiorini di sugello, for the daughter of Salvestro di Giovanni." In the original document, this is then followed by two further entries that relate to Leonardo's financial situation: "He has had 28 fiorini larghi in order to arrange the above-mentioned dowry on our behalf, because he says he does not have the means to pay, and time was elapsing and it was prejudicial to us. In addition he must pay for the colours obtained for him from the Ingesuati which amounts to one and a half fio[rini] larghi: 4 L[ire] 2 sol[di] 4 din[ari]" (MK § 666).

This lengthy document is probably not the actual contract for the commission, but rather an additional business agreement intended to clarify the unusual terms of payment. Other contracts for altarpieces from this same period, such as the contract drawn up with Domenico Ghirlandaio (1449–1494) for an Adoration of the Magi (completed in 1487) for the Ospedale degli Innocenti in Florence, are much more straightforward.

Whenever he began to paint, it seemed that Leonardo trembled, and he never finished any of the works he commenced because, so sublime was his idea of art, he saw faults even in the things that to others seemed miracles.

GIAN PAOLO LOMAZZO, 1590

Adoration of the Magi,
1481/82
Oil on wood, 243 x 246 cm
Florence, Galleria degli Uffizi,
Inv. 1594

The unusual document relating to Leonardo's *Adoration*, on the other hand, details complicated arrangements relating to extra administrative and financial obligations that the artist had to fulfil if he was to receive the agreed sum of 300 *fiorini* once the painting was complete. The financial basis for this payment was one third of the total value of a land holding that the monastery had inherited. This third was valued at 300 *fiorini*, which the monks were to dispose of as follows: 150 *fiorini* were to be used to finance the altarpiece, and the other 150 *fiorini* were to furnish a dowry for a certain Elisabetta, a relative of the donor, within a year. By signing the contract, Leonardo accepted not just the title to one third of the holding and the income this brought with it, but also the not insignificant obligation to put up the dowry for the above-mentioned Elisabetta. As was standard at that time for large-scale altarpieces, Leonardo was also required to bear the costs of his artist's materials himself. Leonardo's fee was thus not paid in the frequently employed manner of periodic instalments, from which he could have defrayed his living expenses and material costs, but was tied up in a legal arrangement that required him to lay out a considerable amount of money in advance. Just four months after signing the first agreement, it emerged that he had insufficient funds at his disposal either to pay for his materials or to make the deposit on the dowry he had contractually agreed to provide. As the two addenda to the above document make painfully clear, the artist was obliged to go back to the monks to borrow money in order to buy paints and put down a first payment towards the dowry.

In the end, even the monks of San Donato a Scopeto themselves realized that the contract they had drawn up with Leonardo did not favour the rapid execution of a large altarpiece. In the agreement they later concluded with Filippino Lippi, they abandoned the complex arrangements of 1481. Instead, the monks sold off the corresponding portion of the property and were consequently in a position to pay the artist the sum of 300 *fiorini* in cash. In retrospect, their revised agreement with Filippino Lippi also helped to exonerate Leonardo; it effectively acknowledged that the stipulations of the 1481 contract had ruled out any possibility of completing the altarpiece. The artist, in other words, was not to blame for the unsatisfactory way in which the commission ended.

Despite its unfinished state, the main features of the composition of the almost square *Adoration*, which today hangs in the Uffizi, are clearly identifiable. Mary and the infant Jesus are seated in the central foreground in front of a small rocky outcrop, out of which two trees are growing. The three kings who followed the Star of Bethlehem on their journey from the East worship before the Child sitting on his mother's lap. In the right-hand foreground, one of the kings has sunk to his knees in reverence; the Child is blessing him as he offers his gift. On the left, a second king is bowing low before the Virgin and Child. The figure kneeling in front of him to the left, looking up with his head raised, is probably that of the third and youngest king. Grouped in a semicircle around the Virgin are also numerous other individuals, including Joseph, who is probably the bearded old man behind the Virgin and who has just removed the lid from the precious vessel presented by the first king. Others belong to the kings' large retinue or are perhaps to be identified as angels.

The figures within the composition thereby display a striking variety of movements and gestures. While the majority of those present devote their undivided attention to the central group of Virgin and Child, some are looking at an apparition in the top part of the picture, probably the Star of Bethlehem, as seen, for example, in Sandro Botticelli's *Adoration of the Magi* (ill. p. 52) painted only shortly before. We are directed towards this imaginary star, or at least towards its light, by a number of gestures in the crowd. Thus two young men – one in the left-hand middle ground and the other on the right of the foot of the nearest tree – are each pointing with the index finger of one hand up to the sky, in order to draw attention to the divine light. This same ges-

Study of a Horse and Rider,
c. 1481
Metalpoint on pale pink prepared paper, 120 x 78 mm
Private Collection

Composition Sketch for the
Adoration of the Magi, **1481**
Pen and ink over metalpoint,
285 x 215 mm
Paris, Musée du Louvre, Cabinet des Dessins, R.F.1978

ture was regularly performed in 15th-century mystery plays based on the story of the Magi and is found in an earlier *Adoration of the Magi* executed by an artist from the workshop of Fra Angelico for the "silver cabinet" in SS Annunziata in Florence. However, Leonardo infuses this gesturing towards the divine light with greater dynamism than the older artist. A comparison with similar "pointing gestures", of the kind employed in Florence a few years earlier by artists in the circle of Domenico Veneziano (*c.* 1410–1461) and Filippo Lippi (*c.* 1406–1469) in portrayals of St John the Baptist, again makes clear the increased dramatic intensity of Leonardo's gestures. On the other hand, the gesture of the hand raised above the head, made by the figure in the right-hand foreground in an attempt to shield himself from the strength of the divine light, appears relatively conventional. This *aposkopein* hand gesture, as it was known, can be found in numerous earlier versions of the Adoration.

Within the group of figures clustered around the central foreground, particular attention should also be paid to Joseph – a character who in many Adorations plays something of a subsidiary role. In Leonardo's composition he is holding the lid of a precious vessel in his right hand. Leonardo thereby indicates that the first king has already presented his gift, gold. According to one legend, the Holy Family accepted the gold, but then gave it to the poor on account of its primarily worldly value. Since the gold, the first gift, has thus evidently already been received, Leonardo's painting must be portraying the moment when the second king presents the Child with his gift of frankincense. Since frankincense was a symbol of Christ's sacrificial death on the cross, its presentation within the *Adoration* may be understood as a reference to the liturgical re-enactment of the Sacrifice taking place in front of the altar during mass. As such, it would have established a direct connection between the subject of the altarpiece and the Eucharist being celebrated beneath it – a connection typically offered by all altarpieces.

In comparison with the figures in the front section of the painting, who are gathered closely around the Virgin and Child and the symbolically charged foreground scene, the people and animals from the kings' entourage in the rear of the composition enjoy considerably more space. As in many paintings of the *Adoration of the Magi*, the ruins of the palace of King David, the Old Testament ancestor of Christ, can be seen in the background. A striking detail here is a number of people busying themselves in front of and on top of the ruins. They have prompted some to conclude that the figures in the left half of background are engaged in rebuilding David's semi-derelict palace. Whatever the case, the two saplings growing on top of the ruins correspond to the two trees behind the Virgin and Child. They may be read – like the rebuilding of David's palace, if this is indeed what is happening – as symbols of the age of peace and grace that was ushered in with the birth of Christ. The larger of the two trees in the middle ground is clinging by its roots to the bare rock, whereby one of these roots seems to establish a link between the tree itself and the head of the Christ Child.

Leonardo may here be drawing upon the story of the Magi as narrated in the popular *Golden Legend* by Jacobus da Voragine, and in particular its discussion of the nature of the star followed by the Wise Men. "Note that the star the Magi saw was a five-fold star", we are told, whereby the fifth of these stars represented Christ himself, interpreted as the "root and stock of David, the bright and morning star". Lastly, the two horses rearing up in the background, whose riders appear at first sight to be engaged in combat, may also be a reference to another medieval legend, according to which the three kings had at one time been bitter enemies. It was only after their miraculous journey and after witnessing the nativity of Christ, the Saviour, that they made peace with each other, like the rest of the world. The violent confrontation of the two horses in the background is thus an allusion to their former enmity, and offers a stark contrast to the era of peace

Detail of Perspective Study for the Background of the Adoration of the Magi, 1481
Pen, ink, traces of metalpoint and white, 165 x 290 mm, Florence, Galleria degli Uffizi, Gabinetto dei Disegni e delle Stampe, Inv. 436 E recto

proclaimed by the Adoration scene in the foreground. In his clear compositional division of foreground and background, Leonardo draws a line between the era before Christ and the age of grace, which began with the birth of Christ and His adoration by all peoples.

In formal terms, Leonardo drew inspiration for his altarpiece from two different but very prominent *Adoration* panels. He took the semicircular arrangement of the foreground figures from Sandro Botticelli's *Adoration of the Magi for Gaspare del Lama* (ill. p. 52), which originally adorned a side altar in Santa Maria Novella in Florence. Leonardo's *Adoration* was destined for a high altar, however, and demanded an emphatically more hierarchical composition in line with its more elevated status. Leonardo may have found such monumentality in Fra Angelico's (*c.* 1395–1455) high altarpiece for San Marco in Florence (ill. p. 53), which in the second half of the 15th century was still considered the paradigm of its genre. Unlike the older work by Fra Angelico, however, Leonardo's altarpiece does not portray a *sacra conversazione*, a relatively static group of saints gathered around the Virgin and Child, but a scene from life: the Adoration of the Child and the presentation of the second gift. Leonardo's *Adoration* thus shows the beginnings of a narrative structure. Narrative themes such as the Adoration and the Annunciation were already finding their way into altarpieces for side chapels from this same period; with Leonardo's *Adoration of the Magi*, they were about to burst onto the stage of the high altar. It was now possible for a *storia*, a narrative in the sense used by Leon Battista Alberti in his treatise on painting, to occupy the supreme position within the hierarchy of religious art – the high altar.

Even more than the unfinished *St Jerome*, the *Adoration* offers us a profound insight into Leonardo's creative process. In several places the painting resembles an enormous sketch. Particularly in the background, where the individual figures are for the most part set down in the barest of detail, the artist reveals the spontaneity of his method, which in many places sees him altering the composition even as he

paints. Leonardo's inventive process – evidently not entirely planned in advance – can be followed in numerous studies from the period around 1481 (ill. p. 50), although only very few of these drawings can be related with absolute certainty to the *Adoration of the Magi* begun in 1481. Just one sketch of the overall composition, the so-called Gallichon drawing, and a perspective study for the background executed probably a little later, can be firmly accepted as preliminary studies for the altarpiece (ill. pp. 50, 51).

The other drawings from this period contain motifs that are no more than similar to those in the *Adoration of the Magi*, and which possibly relate to an *Adoration of the Shepherds* that Leonardo was also planning. The Gallichon drawing is particularly informative. It includes in the background the flights of steps belonging to the former palace of King David, albeit on the right-hand side. The composition as a whole, however, remains far more indebted to earlier 15th-century conventions. Thus the Bethlehem stable is granted a prominent position and is directly linked with the ruins of David's palace. In the second surviving drawing, the roof of the stable is shifted further into the background and only vaguely indicated, while at the same time the rather slapdash perspective of the first drawing is worked out with almost pedantic precision. In the actual painting, the Bethlehem stable is moved to the extreme right-hand edge of the picture (where it is barely recognizable) and its place in the composition is taken by the two trees in the middle ground. Leonardo thereby places the emphasis firmly on the centre of the picture, in the typical fashion of important altarpieces, and imposes a formal hierarchy on the composition as a whole.

Another feature of the *Adoration*, up till now rather ignored, is the striking predominance of certain figural types. Thus the foreground, in particular, is dominated by five bearded old men: two of the three kings, Joseph, an onlooker to the right of the Virgin and the figure on the left-hand edge of the panel. The figural type of the beautiful youth

Sandro Botticelli
Adoration of the Magi for Gaspare del Lama,
c. **1472–1475**
Tempera on wood, 111 x 134 cm
Florence, Galleria degli Uffizi

I was at pains to look out for persons, philosophies, help from the past and from the present, in order to establish particular rules, axiomatic pointers towards a new, expanded understanding of art. For this reason I am profoundly impressed by Leonardo da Vinci and Caspar David Friedrich.

JOSEPH BEUYS, 1974

appears even more frequently, above all in the group behind the Virgin, in the right-hand middle ground and amongst the figures to the left of Joseph. Middle-aged men are almost entirely absent, an omission all the more surprising in view of the fact that the three kings were usually portrayed at three different stages of life. These three kings of three different ages can be seen in numerous works of Florentine painting, from that of Gentile da Fabriano (c. 1370–1427), Lorenzo Monaco (c. 1370–c. 1425) and Masaccio (1401–1428) to Botticelli's *Adoration for Gaspare del Lama*. Leonardo's unusual and one-sided concentration upon two types cannot be adequately explained by the unfinished state of his painting. Rather, Leonardo is continuing the practice – also employed in Verrocchio's workshop – of using certain figural types. Personal preference may also have played a part, for Leonardo took a lifelong pleasure in drawing finely proportioned faces of youths and furrowed countenances of old men, and in contrasting the two types.

The predominance of old men and youths in the *Adoration of the Magi* may also have a third, socio-historical explanation, arising out of the Florentine cult of the Magi. From the 12th century onwards, the Feast of Epiphany, on 6 January, had been marked throughout Europe with a Procession of the Magi, conducted with as much pomp and ceremony as possible. So too in Florence, where the lay confraternity of the "Compagnia de' Magi" was responsible for organizing the Epiphany celebrations. Up to 700 riders took part, parading through the city to commemorate the Adoration of the Christ Child. With the particularly spectacular pageant of 1468, in which the city itself became one enormous stage set, veneration of the Magi reached a peak. During the celebrations, the young members of the fraternity wore masks carved with the faces of their fathers and imitated their actions and habits. The roles of the middle and eldest king were also taken by young men in similar disguises. In their theatrical imitation of the older men, the members of the younger generation demonstrated their aspiration to the social positions still held and fiercely defended by their fathers. In the festive Procession of the Magi and in the re-enactment of the Adoration of the Christ Child, the age dualism in Florentine society was thus made manifest – a dualism with which the polarity between young and old figural types in Leonardo's *Adoration of the Magi* directly corresponds.

It is possible there was even a personal issue at play here. For Leonardo, in 1481 not yet fully established in Florence, had been awarded his largest commission to date probably through the offices of his father. The young artist's struggle to make his professional breakthrough in Florence was thus directly linked to the social position and business contacts of his father, against which Leonardo had little to set. The age dualism of the city of Florence was thus matched by a similar dualism between the artist and his father. Was it to escape this very age dualism, one can't help wondering, that Leonardo had to abandon the *Adoration* unfinished and turn his back on Florence?

Filippino Lippi
Adoration of the Magi, 1496
Tempera on wood, 258 x 243 cm
Florence, Galleria degli Uffizi

Fra Angelico
Altarpiece for San Marco, c. 1438–1440
Tempera on wood, 220 x 227 cm
Florence, Museo di San Marco

In the whole world there is perhaps no other example of a genius so universal, so inventive, so incapable of content-ing himself, so eager for infinity, so naturally intelligent, so far ahead of his century and the centuries which followed. His figures express an incredible sensibility and spirit; they overflow with unexpressed ideas and sensations.

HIPPOLYTE TAINE, 1866

III A fresh start in Milan 1483–1484

Why, towards the end of 1482 or in early 1483, at the age of about 30, Leonardo should have decided to turn his back on Florence and make a new start in Milan has never been fully explained. Probably the most important factor behind his move were the better career prospects offered by the Lombard capital, which with its population of 125,000 was considerably larger than Florence, which numbered around 41,000 inhabitants. Its greater economic importance alone was enough to make the Milanese court of the ruling Sforza family look a more promising place to find work than the city of Florence.

In Milan, Leonardo applied speculatively for well-paid work in not one, but two areas. Not only did he offer to execute an equestrian monument of Francesco Sforza (1401–1466; cf. Ch. IV), but he also tendered his services as an engineer and military architect. Milan was at that time (1483–1484) at war with Venice, and its military ambitions offered attractive scope for a technically gifted artist such as Leonardo. With military expenditure accounting for over 70 per cent of the entire Sforza budget, the prospects of finding employment as an engineer must have struck Leonardo as good. This would explain the memorable letter that he wrote to Ludovico Sforza (1452–1508), in which he applied for the position of court artist (RLW § 1340/MK § 612). Leonardo devotes the main part of the letter, however, to detailing his abilities as a military engineer; only right at the end does he mention his artistic achievements and offer to undertake the equestrian monument mentioned above. It is a striking fact that, amongst his early drawings of military architecture and equipment, those offering a potential application in a battle with Milan's maritime neighbour, Venice, stand out in particular. They include various sketches of fortifications and of machines suitable for use in naval warfare. During this same period Leonardo also made numerous studies relating to surveying equipment for military applications.

Leonardo's first commission in Milan was of an entirely peaceful nature, however. Possibly following a recommendation by Ludovico

Sforza, the Franciscan lay confraternity attached to the church of San Francesco Grande asked the Florentine artist, together with two local artists, the brothers Ambrogio and Evangelista de Predis, to paint a large altarpiece for their recently completed chapel, dedicated to the Feast of the Immaculate Conception. A detailed contract of 25 April 1483 stipulates that the artists were to paint and gild a large retable which joiners and woodcarvers had already completed in 1482 (cf. reconstruction, ill. p. 68), and whose central panel Leonardo was also to paint. Today known as the *Virgin of the Rocks*, this middle panel exists in two versions. The older of the two, executed by Leonardo largely between 1483 and 1484, today hangs in the Louvre in Paris (Cat. XI/ill. p. 57). The second version, which was painted at a later date, partly by Ambrogio de Predis, is housed in the National Gallery in London (Cat. XVI/ill. p. 58). Also in the National Gallery are the two side panels executed by Ambrogio de Predis and portraying two angels making music (ill. pp. 70 and 71).

Several reliefs depicting scenes from the Life of Mary completed the front of this monumental retable, which concluded at the top with a number of prophets and God the Father. A niche in the centre of the altarpiece probably housed what was the true object of devotion within the artistic programme as a whole: a wooden statue of the Virgin and Child – the *Immacolata* – as the symbol of the Immaculate Conception. Leonardo's *Virgin of the Rocks* stood in front of this niche and for 364 days of the year concealed the sculpture of the Virgin behind it. Only on 8 December, the Feast of the Immaculate Conception, was Leonardo's painting lowered by means of a sliding mechanism, bringing the *Immacolata* into view and allowing it be worshipped directly. Thus it seems that Leonardo's *Virgin of the Rocks* in fact served as a sort of screen, behind which was concealed the true object of devotion – the statue of the Virgin, which is mentioned several times in records but which has since vanished. The possibility may not be excluded, however, that the wooden statue and Leonardo's *Virgin of the Rocks*

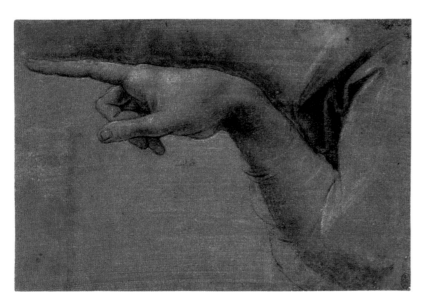

Page 55:
Detail of **The Virgin of the Rocks**, *c.* 1495–1499 and 1506–1508
(ill. p. 58)

Study of a Hand, *c.* 1483
Black chalk heightened with white on dark grey prepared paper, 153 x 220 mm
Windsor Castle, Royal Library
(RL 12520r)

The Virgin of the Rocks (Virgin and Child with the Infant St John and an Angel), 1483–1484/85
Oil on wood, transferred to canvas, 197.3 x 120 cm
Paris, Musée du Louvre, Inv. 777 (MR 320)

were both visible at once: the panel at the lower level of the altarpiece, and the statue one "storey" above it.

Leonardo's middle panel portrays a very youthful Virgin Mary together with the infant St John, the infant Christ and an angel in front of a rocky grotto. Mary is seated in almost the exact centre of the composition and gazes gently down towards the infant St John, her right hand resting on his shoulder as he kneels in prayer. Her left hand seems to hover protectively above the seated infant Jesus. The scene is flanked on the right by an angel, probably Uriel, who is pointing with his right hand towards the infant John. In formal terms, the composition continues to reveal parallels with Florentine art, for example with the very similar arrangement of Christ and John in the marble retable by Mino da Fiesole (1429–1484) in Fiesole cathedral (ill. p. 69). Leonardo's *Study of a Virgin worshipping the Child* (ill. p. 59), which anticipates the composition of *The Virgin of the Rocks* in the disposition of the figures, was probably also executed in Florence.

Despite its references to Florentine forms, the constellation of the figures in the *Virgin of the Rocks* deserves closer examination, since a meeting between John and Christ as infants is rarely depicted in art. Such a meeting is recorded not in the Bible itself, but in pseudepigraphical writings (Protevangelium of James, 17–22). Here it is described how, on the flight into Egypt, Mary and Jesus met Elizabeth and John in the wilderness. The unusual combination of figures in Leonardo's painting and its rugged setting within a rocky landscape, a place of seclusion and refuge, draw upon this encounter during the flight into Egypt and probably also upon medieval accounts of the life of St John.

Seclusion is in fact a central theme of the *Virgin of the Rocks*. Thus the stony ground, consisting in places of thin strata of rock, seems to fall away suddenly and steeply at the front edge of the picture, almost as if the Virgin were sitting on the edge of a chasm that opens up be-

tween the viewer and the painting. In this way, too, Leonardo establishes the remote nature of the location, something reinforced by the rugged rock formations in the middle ground and background. The grotto is thereby divided into two passages of different widths, through which can be seen a distant mountain landscape bathed in light and mist, together with an area of water whose presence at such an altitude comes as something of a surprise – one would not necessarily expect to see a relatively large body of water amidst such rocky heights. A number of these elements may carry a very broad symbolism: the passage on the left, for example, leading through the rocks towards the water, might be intended to represent the *vena di aqua bellissima* (vein of most beautiful water), a metaphorical image through which, in the 14th century, the Dominican Domenico Cavalca sought to convey the purity of the Virgin. Indeed, water in general stood for the purity of Mary. In the second version of the *Virgin of the Rocks*, in particular, the body of water in the background has grown to a considerable size, to the extent that – even at this altitude – it can be called a sea (ill. pp. 64/65). This, too, may be intended as a reference to Marian symbolism: earlier exegetists derived the name "Mary" from the Latin word for sea, *mare*, and just as all rivers flow into the sea, so divine Grace flows into Mary. The divide opening up in front of Mary may be similarly interpreted with reference to patristic sources and contemporary Franciscan literature: this abyss was seen as the impenetrable depths of the great ocean of prehistory, from which all water comes and to which all water returns.

Marian symbolism may also underlie the unusual rock formations of the background, cleft into two passages. It is possible that they refer to similar topoi (stock themes) in the liturgy and to metaphors used to describe Mary in the Bible. In the Song of Songs (1:14), for example, Mary is described as a "dove ... in the clefts of the rock" (*columba in foraminibus petrae*) and "in the cavities of walls" (*in caverna maceriae*). The Mother of God was also considered to be a "rock cleft not by human

The Virgin of the Rocks (Virgin and Child with the Infant St John and an Angel), *c.* **1495–1499 and 1506–1508**
Oil on poplar (parqueted), 189.5 x 120 cm
London, National Gallery, Inv. 1093

Studies of a Virgin worshipping the Child, *c.* **1482–1485**
Pen and ink over preliminary pencil drawing, 195 x 162 mm
New York, The Metropolitan Museum of Art, Rogers Fund, 1917 (17.142.1)

Study for the Head of a Girl, 1483
Silverpoint on brownish prepared paper, 182 x 159 mm
Turin, Biblioteca Reale, Inv. 15572r

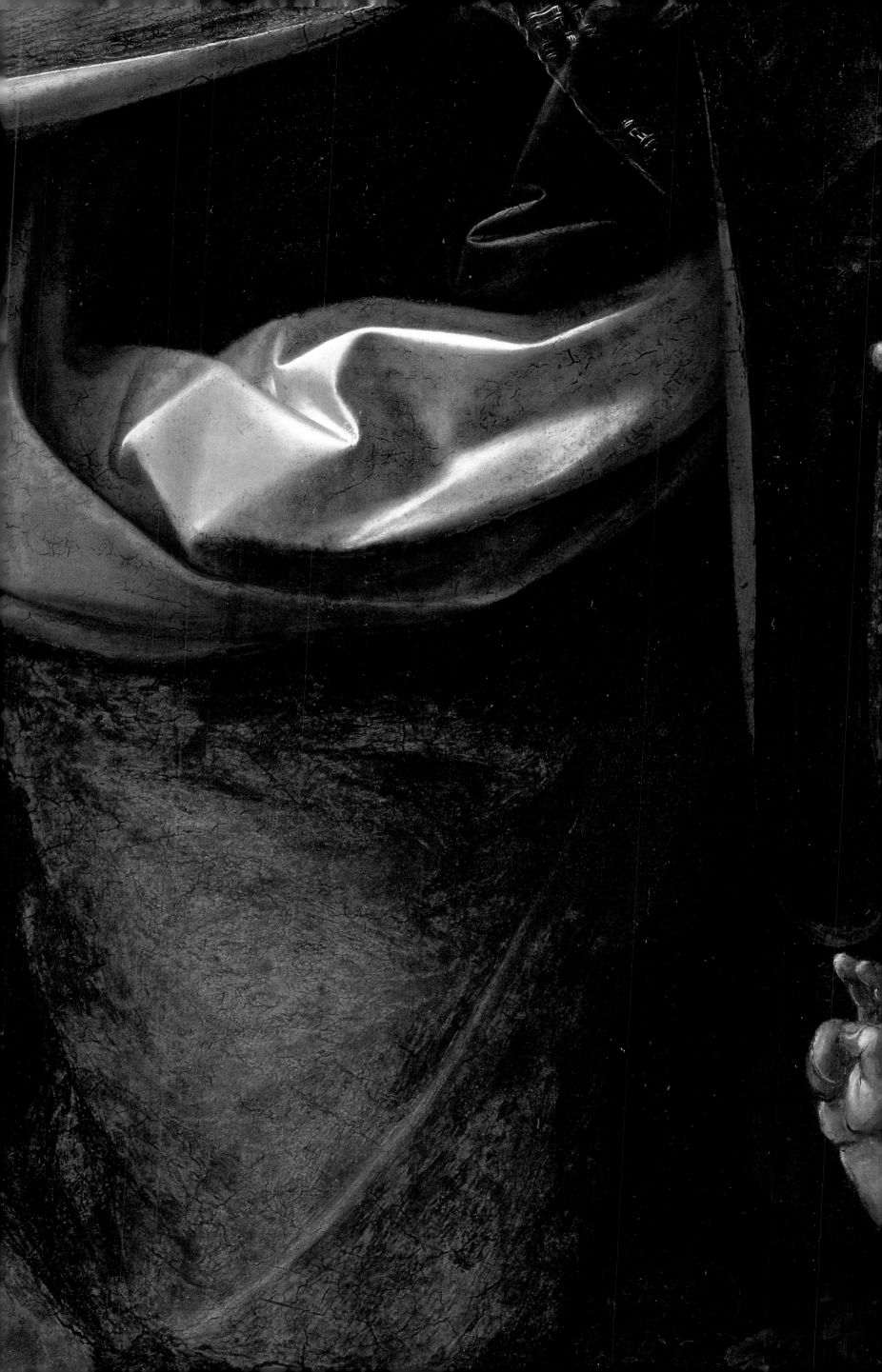

But before we go any further, we must say a little more about Leonardo's personality and talents. The many gifts that Nature bestowed upon him concentrated themselves primarily in his eye. Hence, although capable of all things, he appeared great above all as a painter. He did not rely simply upon the inner impulses of his innate, inestimable talent; he permitted no arbitrary, random stroke of the brush; everything had to be deliberate and considered. From the pure proportions to which he devoted so much research, to the strangest monsters that he compiled out of contradictory figures, everything had to be both natural and rational.

JOHANN WOLFGANG VON GOETHE, 1787

IV Beginnings as court artist in Milan 1485–1494

On the basis of payment receipts, we know that Leonardo finished the *Virgin of the Rocks* in late 1484 or early 1485. Even though he had thus completed his first larger-scale painting in Milan admirably on schedule, the artist appears to have received no other commissions for paintings at this stage. Even his hopes of a position as court artist, conveyed in his letter to Ludovico Sforza, would be fulfilled only some years later. Precisely what professional activities Leonardo pursued in the mid to late 1480s in Milan, and how he kept his head financially above water, are questions that remain largely unexplained to this day. All we know for certain about this period is that it saw him designing war machines, some of them more fantastical than practical. He also drew weapons of all different kinds, fortifications, complex defence systems, siege equipment and more besides.

Amongst the curiosities of this phase are heavily armoured vehicles, whose immense weight would have all but prevented them from moving. Other ideas seem more immediately dangerous, such as his suggestion that the firepower of smaller cannon could be increased by using what was effectively grapeshot and an automated loading system. Positively gruesome are the horse-drawn chariots armoured with scythes, with which the enemy could literally be mown down. Leonardo copied at least one device of this kind from a contemporary military treatise, Roberto Valturio's (c. 1405/15–1475) De re militari of 1472, and drew it several times (ill. p. 74). Not without irony, however, did he accompany his drawing with a warning that this kind of equipment could do just as much damage to one's own troops as to those of the enemy.

Leonardo did not restrict his skills as a draughtsman to war machines alone. During this same period he was also trying his hand at architecture, producing designs for churches (ill. p. 75) and endeavouring to impress the authorities in charge of the construction of Milan Cathedral with his designs. There are even records of a number of payments made to the Florentine artist from July 1487 onwards, in connection with the building of a model for the crossing-dome (*tiburio*) of the still unfinished cathedral. Leonardo's proposals drew little response, however; the contracts went to local Lombard architects who were either better qualified or better connected. More important, in terms of architectural history, are Leonardo's numerous designs for centrally planned buildings – even if none of them, it seems, got further than the drawing-board. They nevertheless reflect the architectural debate surrounding churches on centralized plans, which was current in the late 15th century and which would culminate, just a few years later, in the proposed new designs for St Peter's in Rome.

Only towards the end of the 1480s does Leonardo seem to have returned more productively to the visual arts. The *Litta Madonna*, a small-format representation of the Virgin and Child, may have been executed at this time or a little later, although its attribution to Leonardo, always contentious, can no longer be upheld (Cat. XIV/ill. p. 76). The overall hardness of the contours of the Virgin and Child, and the comparatively mundane atmosphere of the background, point instead to one of Leonardo's pupils, Giovanni Antonio Boltraffio (1467–1516), to whom the master entrusted either the entire execution of the painting, or at least its completion. Two drawings from Boltraffio's hand serve to confirm this suspicion. Leonardo was nevertheless directly involved in the original design of the *Litta Madonna*, as evidenced by two authenticated preparatory studies (ill. p. 77).

That Leonardo should supply the designs for smaller Madonna paintings without always executing them entirely himself was probably bound up with the fact that, around 1490, he was preoccupied with more important things. Over a period of time somewhere between 1484 and 1494 – it is not possible to be more precise – the artist was engaged upon his important and most difficult project to date, the Sforza monument – the largest equestrian statue in the modern age. The monument, which was to be much bigger than life size and cast in bronze, was intended by Ludovico Sforza to commemorate the mil-

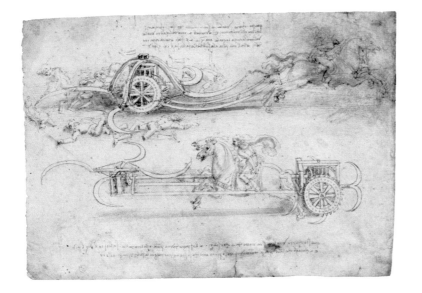

Page 73:
Detail of **Portrait of an Unknown Woman (La Belle Ferronière)**, *c.* 1490–1495
(ill. p. 93)

Scythed Chariot, *c.* 1483–1485
Pen and ink, 210 x 290 mm
Turin, Biblioteca Reale,
Inv. 15583r

Page 75:
Studies of a Centrally planned Building,
c. 1487–1490
Pen and ink, 233 x 162 mm
Paris, Bibliothèque de l'Institute de France, Codex Ashburnham 1875/1 (Ms. B 2184), fol. 5v

I visualized how Leonardo would draw technology today, if he were alive now [...] and indeed tried [...] as far as I could, to render this visible.

JOSEPH BEUYS, 1979

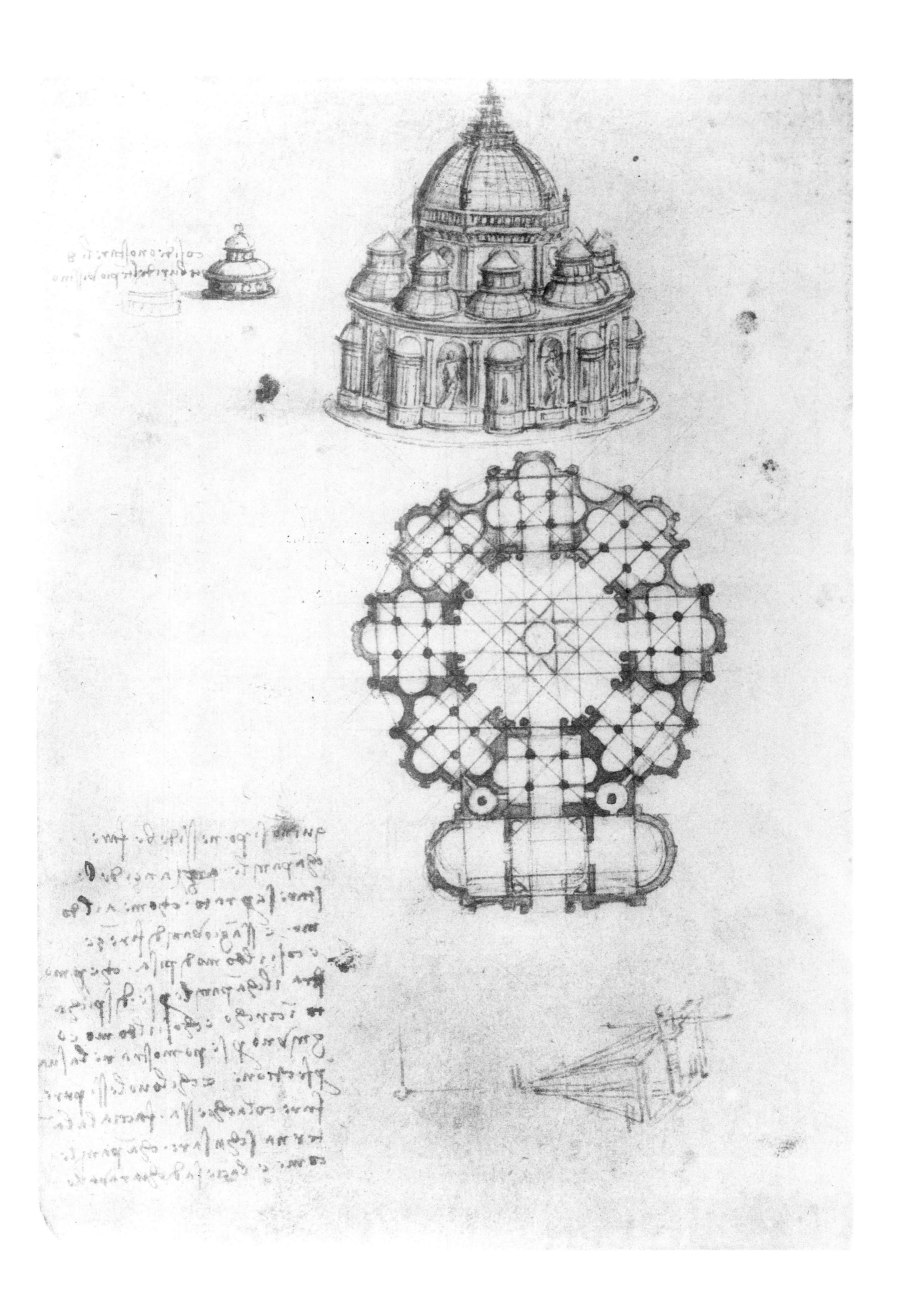

itary successes of his father, Francesco Sforza, and of course to cast his own achievements in an equally impressive light. Francesco had distinguished himself as a general in the 1430s and lent his military support to the then Duke of Milan, Filippo Maria Visconti (1392–1447). In 1441 Francesco Sforza allied himself with Milan's ruling Visconti dynasty yet more closely by marrying Bianca Maria (*c.* 1424–1468), the duke's daughter.

When Filippo Maria Visconti died a few years later, in 1447, Francesco Sforza used the resulting power vacuum to set himself up as ruler of Milan. As the son-in-law of the deceased Filippo Maria Visconti, who had left no legitimate male heirs, Francesco was officially proclaimed Duke of Milan in 1450 and went on to found a new dynasty to succeed the Visconti. Following Francesco's own death, the title passed to his first-born son, Galeazzo Maria (1444–1476), and when he was murdered in 1476, he was succeeded in turn by his son Gian Galeazzo Sforza (1469–1494), who was still a minor. Since Gian Galeazzo was not yet in a position to govern in his own name, the reins of power were seized by his uncle, Ludovico Sforza. When, in 1494, Gian Galeazzo mysteriously departed this life, Ludovico was officially able to declare himself sole ruler of Milan. Prior to 1494, therefore, Ludovico il Moro, Leonardo's patron and employer, was not the rightful Duke of Milan, since this title belonged to his nephew Gian Galeazzo, who stood in the direct line of male succession. Ludovico was thus faced with the problem of legitimizing his claim to power, which was flawed in two genealogical respects: firstly, his father Francesco did not stand in direct line of male succession from the Visconti dukes; and secondly, he himself, Ludovico, was not the first-born son of the Sforza family, but merely the uncle of the true Duke of Milan, who died young in circumstances never fully explained. These genealogical weaknesses led him to focus his cultural policy largely upon demonstrating the magnificence of the still young Sforza dynasty. The products of this policy included such vainglorious literary monuments as

Giovanni Simonetta's (*c.* 1410/20–1491) *De gestis Francisci Sphortiae* (cf. Ch. V), an extensive building programme in Milan and Pavia, the commissioning of the *Last Supper* and above all the equestrian monument to Francesco Sforza, which was intended to do no less than redefine its genre.

Plans for an equestrian monument were first mooted in the early 1470s, and by November 1473 they were already taking concrete shape. In a letter from Galeazzo Maria Sforza to Bartolomeo da Cremona dating from this same year, we find the first mention of a life-size equestrian statue to be sited in front of the Castello Sforzesco, the Sforza's castle in Milan: "For we would like to have an image [*imagine*] of our Most Illustrious Lord and father made in his good memory, of bronze and mounted on horseback, and we want to erect it in some part of our Milan castle, either on the entrenchment facing the piazza or somewhere else where it will be seen to advantage. We wish and enjoin you to search in our city for a master who can execute this work and cast it in metal, and if no such master is to be found in our city, we wish you to investigate and find out whether in another city or elsewhere there is a master who knows how to do it. And he must make the image and the horse as well as can possibly be imagined. The image must be as big as His Lordship and the horse of a goodly size. And if such a master is to be found, send us news, and let us know how much the costs, including the metal, the work and all other things, will amount to. And we wish you to search in Rome, Florence and all other cities where the master might be found who could carry out this work successfully."

Actual work on the monument, at first planned only in life size ("as big as His Lordship") and hence on a modest scale, was repeatedly postponed, however, since there were no competent artists to be found either in Upper Italy or elsewhere. Following the murder of Galeazzo Maria in 1476 and the temporary exiling of Ludovico Sforza from 1477 to 1479, the project came to a complete standstill.

Giovanni Antonio Boltraffio (?),
after a design by Leonardo
Litta Madonna, *c.* 1490
Tempera (and oil?) on wood,
transferred to canvas, 42 x 33 cm
St Petersburg, Hermitage, Inv. 249

Study of the Head of a
Woman, *c.* 1490
Silverpoint on greenish prepared
paper, 180 x 168 mm
Paris, Musée du Louvre, Cabinet
des Dessins

In painting he brought to the technique
of colouring in oils a way of darkening
the shadows which has enabled modern
painters to give great vigour and relief
to their figures.

GIORGIO VASARI, 1568

As the Sforza family consolidated its power in the 1480s, however, the idea of an equestrian monument must have acquired a new relevance, to the point that Leonardo could refer to it in the speculative letter of application that he addressed to Ludovico (cf. Ch. IV): "Moreover, work could be undertaken on the bronze horse which will be to the immortal glory and eternal honour of the auspicious memory of His Lordship your father, and of the illustrious house of Sforza" (MK § 612). A good ten years later, around 1495, Leonardo would even claim that Ludovico had invited him to come to Milan to execute the monument (RLW § 1347).

There is no reliable evidence, however, to prove that Leonardo was indeed appointed specifically to build the monument, or even that he started working on the project soon after his arrival in Milan, namely in 1483 or 1484. The first authentic document relating to Leonardo's work on the monument dates from as late as 22 July 1489 and only suggests that all is not well. The Florentine envoy in Milan, Piero Alamanno, inquired in a letter to Lorenzo de' Medici whether there were artists in Florence who would be able to see the colossal monument through to completion, since Leonardo does not seem to be capable of it: "It is the intention of His Lordship Ludovico to erect a worthy monument to his father, and he has already instructed Leonardo da Vinci to produce the model for a very large bronze horse and on it the figure of Duke Francesco in full armour. Since His Excellency would like to make something truly outstanding [*in superlativo grado*], I was advised by him to write to you and to ask you to send him one or two artists from Florence who are accomplished in this field. For although the Duke has commissioned Leonardo da Vinci to do the work, it seems to me that he is not confident that he knows how to do it."

It is possible that Leonardo was to lose responsibility for the project or – if we interpret the letter a little more optimistically – was to be assigned some experienced assistants. Whatever the case, he must have broken off work on the monument, because on 23 April 1490 he wrote

in a notebook that he had "recommended the horse" (RLW § 720). And indeed, over the next two years the artist worked intensively on designs for the monumental work, and above all on the technical aspects of casting it in bronze (ill. pp. 80, 81).

Finally, in 1493 he completed an enormous clay model of the horse, over seven metres (!) in height, which was exhibited that same year during the festivities to mark the marriage of Bianca Maria Sforza, Ludovico's niece, to Emperor Maximilian I (reg. 1468–1519), when it formed part of the decorations in the Corte Vecchio in Milan. An ode composed by the court poet Baldassare Taccone in 1493 describes the work thus:

> "See in the Corte the colossal horse,
> To be cast in bronze in memory of the father:
> I firmly believe that Greece and Rome
> Never saw a greater work of art.
> Just see how beautiful this horse is;
> Leonardo made it single-handedly,
> A fine sculptor, painter, geometer:
> His rare genius sent from Heaven.
> It was always the wish of His Lordship [Ludovico],
> But it was not begun earlier
> For a Leonardo had not yet been found,
> He who now shapes it so well
> That everyone who sees it is amazed.
> And if one compares him with Phidias,
> With Myron, Scopas and Praxiteles,
> One can but say: Never on earth was a work more beautiful."

Alongside the usual panegyric, Taccone's poem contains a number of interesting references. It speaks of a "colossal" horse (*gran colosso*) and thus indirectly of the revision the project has undergone – in Galeazzo

**Allegory of Statecraft
(Justice and Prudence),**
c. 1490–1494
Pen and ink, 205 x 285 mm
Oxford, The Governing Body,
Christ Church, Inv. JBS 18r

*[...] art and scientific genius came
together in Leonardo's spirit.*

THOMAS MANN, 1936

Maria Sforza's letter of 1473 it was envisaged as only life-sized (see above). The significant increase in the size of the monument can thus be attributed to Ludovico, whose craving for public admiration clearly surpassed even that of his deceased brother. Revealing, too, is Taccone's description of Leonardo as a geometer (*geometra*), clearly a reference to the artist's "scientific" studies (cf. Ch. V). Lastly, the poem also offers us a guide to the dating of the monument, for Taccone speaks in the present tense of the sculpting of the monument. The clay model had evidently only just been finished or was not far off completion.

On 20 December 1493 Leonardo made another important note in the manuscript later known as the Codex Madrid II, indicating some of the serious technical difficulties into which the project had run. The pit in which the horse was to be cast, and which thus had to be at least as deep as the horse was tall, had hit the water table (CM II, fol. 151v). Shortly after this, therefore, Leonardo must have decided to cast the horse lying horizontally in the pit, not standing upright. In view of this and other problems, the ambitious project got little further than the clay model, and in 1494 the bronze earmarked for the monument was appropriated to make cannon instead. The need to fight the French, who had marched into Italy as Ludovico's allies and had subsequently become his enemies, meant that there were now more urgent uses for the metal. The largest monument ever designed to honour the memory of a soldier and general fell victim, characteristically, to the demands of another war.

For some years the clay model for the Sforza monument aroused the curiosity and admiration of guests and others passing through Milan, but after the arrival of the French troops in 1499 it fell into the hands of mercenaries who had little interest in art. It was used, so the story goes, for target practice by the archers, whereby it was largely ruined and eventually destroyed altogether. Like the final execution of the bronze equestrian monument, its clay model thus also fell

victim to the consequences of war. Still surviving, however, are numerous sketches and preparatory studies from Leonardo's hand, which convey a lively impression of the different stages and the technical challenges of the project (ill. pp. 80, 81). Thus, besides a drawing for a – strangely surrealist – ironwork mould for casting the head, there are also numerous studies relating to the final appearance, movements and proportions of the horse. The most impressive of these studies shows a rider on a horse rearing up on its hind legs. Lying beneath it is an opponent who has clearly fallen to the ground and is holding up his shield in his right hand in an attempt to ward off further attack. The motif of the rearing horse and a slain enemy lying on the ground beneath it derives from antiquity: Xenophon (4th century BC), in his writings on horsemanship and cavalry, describes it as a compositional formula of particular dignity (*dexileos*).

The same motif also appeared on antique coins, where it carried imperial and military connotations (ill. p. 159); such coins were widely available in the 15th century, and we know that Leonardo was familiar with them. Through the *dexileos* motif familiar from Greek literature and numismatics, it was attempted to position the political and military ambitions of 15th-century patrons within the grand tradition of antiquity, whose rulers and generals were seen as outstanding individuals worthy of emulation. This reference to an antique tradition must have been especially attractive to Galeazzo Maria Sforza, and later to his brother Ludovico, since the dynasty founded by their father was still young and thus relatively lacking in tradition. An equestrian monument aligning them with classical antiquity would help make up for this genealogical deficiency.

The construction of a horse rearing up on two legs – especially in view of the enormous scale of the project – would have posed considerable problems with regard to the stability of the statue. In a second planning phase, therefore, Leonardo decided to use the less dramatic option of a horse striding forwards. The more animated and artistical-

After Leonardo
Designs for the Sforza Monument
Copperplate engraving,
217 x 159 mm
London, British Museum,
Inv. B.M.5–P.v.181.3

Donatello
Equestrian Monument of the Condottiere Erasmo da Nanni (so-called Gattamelata), 1444–1453
Bronze, 340 x 390 cm
Padua, Piazza del Santo

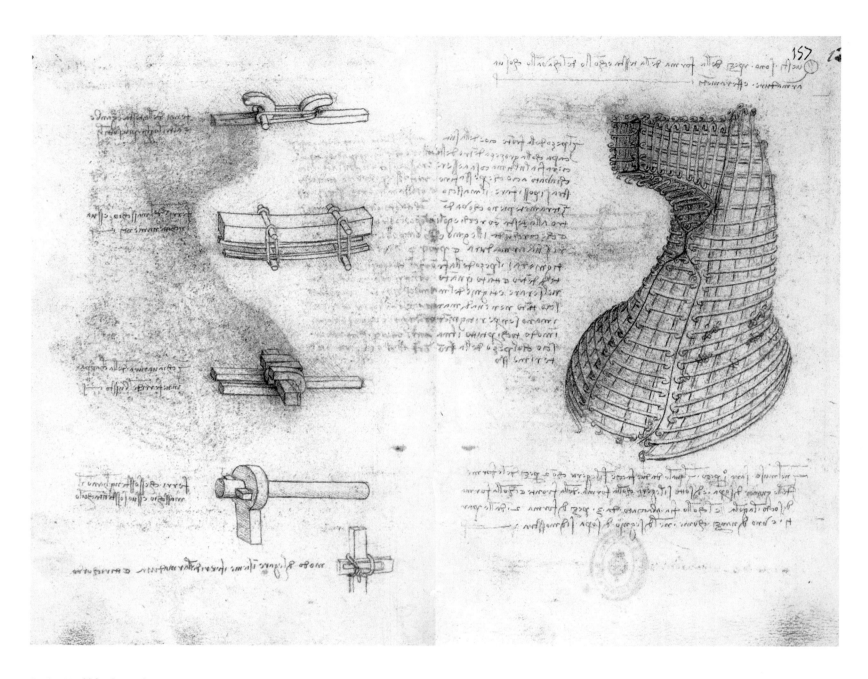

**Casting Mould for the Head
of the Sforza Horse**, *c.* 1491–1493
Red chalk, 210 x 290 mm
Madrid, Biblioteca Nacional,
Codex Madrid II (Ms. 8936),
ff. 156v–157r

There have even been some to say […] that Leonardo had no intention of finishing it when he started. This was because it was so large that it proved an insoluble problem to cast it in one piece; and one can realize why, the outcome being what it was, many came to the conclusion they did, seeing that so many of his works remained unfinished.

GIORGIO VASARI, 1568

ly more interesting *dexileos* motif thus remained simply an ideal, one that Leonardo would take up once more in his Trivulzio monument (cf. Ch. IX), but which would only finally be translated into sculpture by the artists of the 17th and 18th century. By adopting a walking horse, the project now resembled such monuments as the so-called *Regisole* in Pavia, an antique equestrian statue that Leonardo went to look at in person around 1490. The artist thus made a return, in this second phase, to a more traditional formal solution.

Equestrian monuments derive their significance not only from their size, the rank of the person being venerated and the artistry of their design, but also from the site on which they are erected. The most famous and largest equestrian statues of Leonardo's day – the *Gattamelata* by Donatello (1386–1466; ill. p. 91) in Padua, and the still unfinished *Colleoni* by Andrea del Verrocchio in Venice – were firmly embedded within a religious context by their function and location. As cenotaphs, respectively commemorating the deaths of the distinguished generals Gattamelata and Colleoni, both were sited directly outside churches, the *Gattamelata* beside St Anthony's basilica in Padua and the *Colleoni* in front of the Dominican church of SS Giovanni e Paolo in Venice. From Piero Alamanno's letter of 22 July 1489, cited earlier, we know that the equestrian monument for Francesco Sforza was also intended as a *sepultura* (sepulchral monument). But in contrast to the two equestrian statues in Padua and Venice, this *sepultura* was never intended for an ecclesiastical setting; rather, it was to be sited either inside the grounds of the Castello Sforzesco, seat of power of the Sforza dukes, or on top of the outer fortification wall, on the side facing the city. The decision to erect the Sforza monument in front of the ducal palace and directly facing the city of Milan was clearly a deliberate break with post-antique tradition. Far more than simply a memorial to the dead, the monument was to be a grandiose display of Sforza grandeur. The choice of location for the Sforza monument was, in itself, a supreme demonstration of power.

This desire to reinforce the legitimacy of the young Sforza dynasty and cast it in a glittering light expressed itself not just in plans for spectacular monuments, which offered a welcome challenge for an ambitious artist, but also extended to smaller-scale and today less well-known areas of activity. As court artist from 1487 to 1490, Leonardo was also in charge of the design and often, too, the organization of theatrical productions and court festivities. In January 1490, for example, he designed the artistic decorations and necessary technical equipment for the "Festa del Paradiso" staged on the occasion of the marriage of Isabella of Aragon (1470–1524) to Gian Galeazzo Sforza. This pageant was written by the court poet Bernardo Bellincioni (1452–1492), who like Leonardo had also come to Milan from Florence.

A description of the "Festa del Paradiso" can be found in a collection of Bellincioni's poetry, published in book form in 1493. This description, which together with Bellincioni's ode to the *Portrait of Cecilia Gallerani* (see below) marks the first time that Leonardo's name is mentioned in print, sheds light on the activities on which the artist was engaged at the Milanese court: "The following small work, composed by Mr Bernardo Bellincioni for a pageant or rather a performance entitled 'Paradise', was commissioned by Ludovico in praise of the Duchess of Milan. It is called 'Paradise' because, with the assistance of the great talent and skill of Leonardo da Vinci of Florence, it presented Paradise with all the seven planets orbiting around it. And the planets were portrayed by men in the manner described by the poets. And these planets all spoke in praise of the aforementioned Duchess […]". The primary task of the court artist was thus to cast the virtues of the members of the ruling dynasty in a favourable light and make them the subject of a piece of theatrical entertainment. The artist was thereby expected to include impressive artistic and technical effects. Anyone hoping for a successful and lasting engagement as court artist in Milan, therefore, had to bring with them a certain degree of technical expertise.

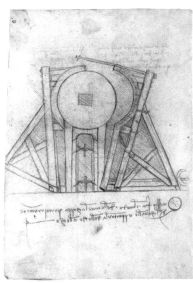

Study for the Sforza Monument,
c. 1488/89
Metalpoint on blue prepared paper,
148 x 185 mm
Windsor Castle, Royal Library
(RL 12358)

Study of the Wooden Framework with Casting Mould for the Sforza Horse, *c. 1491–1493*
Red chalk, 210 x 146 mm
Madrid, Biblioteca Nacional, Codex Madrid II (MS 8936), fol. 155v

It was probably within the context of such pageants and performances that Leonardo also devised a number of allegories, in which, for example, Ludovico il Moro plays the role of protector of the official but still underage ruler of Milan, his nephew Gian Galeazzo Sforza. Leonardo thereby provided the artistic backdrop to Ludovico's political ambitions, inventing complex allegories that managed to captivate the young Gian Galeazzo even as they illustrated his calculating uncle's thirst for power. In one of these allegories (ill. p. 78), Gian Galeazzo appears in the centre of the picture as a cockerel sitting on a cage (the cockerel, *galetto* in Italian, is a play upon his name, Galeazzo). Lunging towards him from the right is a mob made up of foxes, a bird of prey and a horned satyr-like creature. To the left of centre, Ludovico is represented by the figures of not just one, but two Virtues. Thus he is both Justice (*giustizia*, with the attribute of the sword) and Prudence (*prudenza*, with a mirror). Prudence is swinging above her head a snake (the traditional *biscia viscontea*) and a sort of broom or brush, both heraldic symbols of the Sforza family. Prudence is holding her left hand protectively over the cockerel, which is behind her back. Ludovico in allegorical form is thus protecting the *galetto* Gian Galeazzo from the mob approaching from the right.

As artist to the Sforza court and its festivities, Leonardo was once again in demand as a painter. The creative talents that he had previously brought to pageants and allegories found their most impressive expression in his *Portrait of Cecilia Gallerani* (Cat. XIII/ill. p. 79), in which Leonardo broke away from the compositional format prevailing in Upper Italian portraiture of his day (cf. portrait by de Predis, ill. p. 86). Thus he did not adopt the profile view typically employed in nuptial portraits, since he did not have to portray Cecilia as a bride, but as the mistress of Ludovico Sforza (see below). Leonardo also distanced himself from the traditional, rather static pose in which head and upper body face the same way. In the *Portrait of Cecilia Gallerani*, the two are angled in different directions: the upper body is turned to the

left, the head to the right. The painting thereby corresponds to the dynamic style of portraiture that Leonardo was already working towards in his *Portrait of Ginevra de'Benci* (Cat. VII/ill. p. 37) and which is explicitly formulated in his treatise on painting (TPL 357). This desire to infuse the portrait with a sense of movement emerges not only in the positioning of Cecilia's head and body, but also in the dynamic pose of the ermine, which echoes that of the young woman. Cecilia's elegantly curved but at the same time somewhat overly large hand in turn corresponds with the figure of the ermine.

The presence of the ermine within the composition is on the one hand an allusion to Cecilia's surname, since the sound of Galle-rani is reminiscent of the Greek word for ermine, *galée*. On the other hand, the ermine was also a symbol of purity and moderation, for according to legend it abhorred dirt and ate only once a day. Leonardo refers specifically to these qualities of the ermine in his writings, where he makes notes on the allegorical significance of other animals, too (RLW § 1234). The legendary purity of the ermine is also the starting-point for a pen drawing probably dating from around 1490 (ill. p. 82). In this allegory, Leonardo illustrates the traditional belief that an ermine would rather be killed than sully its white fur in dirty water as it flees.

From the late 1480s onwards, moreover, the ermine could also be read as an allusion to Ludovico Sforza, who used it as one of his emblems. In the figurative sense, therefore, this portrait shows Ludovico, in the shape of his symbolic animal, being tenderly stroked in the sitter's arms. The comparatively complex symbolism of this portrait, and the delicate situation it portrays, have their explanation in the fact that the young woman was Ludovico Sforza's favourite mistress. Born Cecilia Bergamini in 1473, at the age of ten she was betrothed (*pro verba*) to Giovanni Stefano Visconti. This betrothal was dissolved in 1487. Not long afterwards, probably in 1489, Cecilia became the mistress of Ludovico Sforza, who for his part had been betrothed to Beatrice d'Este

[…] so that he seemed to his contemporaries to be the possessor of some unsanctified and secret wisdom.

WALTER PATER, 1873

The Ermine as a Symbol of Purity, *c.* 1490
Pen and ink, dia. 91 mm
Cambridge, The Fitzwilliam Museum

Page 83:
Portrait of Cecilia Gallerani (Lady with an Ermine),
1489/90
Oil on walnut, 55 x 40.5 cm
Cracow, Muzeum Narodowe,
Czartoryski Collection, Inv. 134

(1475–1497) since 1480. The official solemnization of Ludovico's marriage to Beatrice d'Este seems to have been delayed from 1490, as originally planned, to 1491 as a consequence of Ludovico's affair with Cecilia. Thus the Ferrarese envoy in Milan, Giacomo Trotti, wrote in November 1490 that Ludovico was not at all looking forward to the arrival of his lawful bride Beatrice, for his mistress Cecilia was as lovely as a flower and, moreover, pregnant. In order to avoid angering his future wife Beatrice, in February 1491 Cecilia was removed from the ducal place as a precaution and taken to a new location, where on 3 May she gave birth to a son, Cesare. There is documentary evidence that the present portrait, which was probably finished quite some time earlier, remained in her possession and perhaps served to remind her of the premarital and extramarital pleasures she and Ludovico shared. Perhaps it was also intended to make up, in some small way, for the inconveniences that Cecilia had to suffer in view of the impending marriage between Ludovico and Beatrice.

Of the nuptial and prenuptial conflicts and pleasures that possibly find expression in Leonardo's *Portrait of Cecilia Gallerani* there is naturally no mention in the panegyrical poetry written for the court. Before his death in 1492, for example, court poet Bernardo Bellincioni composed the following effusive ode to Cecilia and her portrait:

"The poet: 'Nature, who stirs your wrath, who arouses your envy?'
Nature: 'It is Vinci, who has painted one of your stars!
Cecilia, today so very beautiful, is the one
Beside whose beautiful eyes the sun appears as a dark shadow.'

The poet: 'All honour to you [Nature], even if in his picture
She seems to listen and not talk.
Think only, the more alive and more beautiful she is,
The greater will be your glory in future times.

Be grateful therefore to Ludovico, or rather
To the talent [*ingegno*] and hand of Leonardo
Which allows you to be part of posterity.

Everyone who sees her – even if too late
To see her alive – will say: that suffices for us
To understand what is nature and what art.'"

In his fictitious dialogue, Bellincioni takes up the popular theme of the rivalry between nature and the artist, who tries to compete with nature in his works. To this he adds the usual references to the beauty of the lady in the portrait and the generosity of the patron, and in this case also implies that only in the painting are we seeing the sitter behave in the appropriate manner for young women. Only in her portrait, in other words, is she no longer talking (*favella*) but listening! Apart from this joking allusion to ideal female behaviour, which apparently consists of polite silence, Bellincioni's poem also sheds light on contemporary attitudes towards the function of the portrait: it was to hand down a likeness of the young woman for posterity.

Alongside the *Portrait of Cecilia Gallerani*, Leonardo's early works as court painter also include the so-called *Belle Ferronière* (Cat. XV/ill. p. 101), whose attribution to Leonardo is today rarely doubted. In compositional terms, the painting is closely related to a portrait type found across northern Italy, in which a stone parapet separates the viewer from the pictorial space. This same type surfaces in the works of Antonello da Messina (*c.* 1430–1479/ill. p. 87) and Giorgione (1477–1510), for example, and is ultimately indebted to earlier Flemish models. Uncertainty continues to reign, however, over the dating of the portrait and the identity of the sitter. The portrait may show Lucrezia Crivelli, another of Ludovico Sforza's mistresses. If this is indeed the case, then the following lines by another contemporary poet (probably Antonio Tebaldeo) can be related to the painting:

Ambrogio de Predis (?)
Portrait of a Young Woman in Profile, *c.* **1490** (?)
Oil on wood, 51 x 34 cm
Milan, Pinacoteca Ambrosiana

Painting is the finest of all the mechanical arts, and the noblest. It creates more wondrous things than poetry or sculpture. The painter deploys shading and colour and marries them with the gift of precise observation. He must be a master of everything, for everything interests him. The painter is a philosopher of natural science, an architect and a skilful dissector. In this is rooted the excellence of his portrayal of every part of the human body. This skill was some time ago developed and brought to near perfection by Leonardo da Vinci.

GERONIMO CARDANO, 1551

"How well high Art here corresponds to Nature!
Da Vinci could, as so often, have depicted the soul.
But he did not, so that the painting might be a good likeness.
For the Moor alone possessed her soul in his love.
She who is meant is called Lucretia, and to her the gods
Gave everything with a lavish hand.
How rare her form! Leonardo painted her, the Moor loved her:
The one, first among painters, the other, first among princes.
Surely the painter has offended Nature and the high goddesses
With his picture. It galls her the latter that the human hand is
capable of so much,
The former that a figure that should quickly perish
Has been granted immortality.
He did it for the love of the Moor, for which the Moor protects
him.
Both gods and men fear to upset the Moor."

The poet here reflects upon the rivalry between art and nature even more clearly than Bellincioni. He also stresses the gracious patronage bestowed by Ludovico Sforza (also known as Ludovico il Moro, "the Moor"), who alone is able to protect the painter from Nature, whose jealously has been aroused by his art. The poet also raises the issue of the portrayal of the soul, a central aspect of the individual portrait of the modern age. While affirming that Leonardo could easily have portrayed the sitter's soul, the poet emphasizes that it belongs to the patron and ruler, in this case Ludovico il Moro, who as absolute ruler and as a man was accustomed to commanding the bodies and souls of his mistresses.

Amongst the portraits associated with Leonardo's first period in Milan is lastly the *Portrait of a Musician* (Cat. XII/ill. p. 88), whose attribution to Leonardo is the subject of controversy, however. Compared with the more elegant portraits of the *Belle Ferronière* and *Cecilia*

Gallerani, the painting of the young man looking out of the picture towards the right seems rather wooden, partly owing to the fact that the musician's upper body is facing in the same direction as his gaze. But despite the rather less dynamic pose of the *Musician*, both it and the two other portraits from the Milan period convey a certain atmosphere, one that arises out of their subtle shading and that would shortly be encapsulated in the term *sfumato* (cf. Ch. VII and IX). Contours and outlines hereby begin to dissolve as objects no longer rely on crystalline focus and sharp-edged definition to convey themselves to the viewer. The portrait now takes its meaning less from the realism with which it portrays its sitter than from its constitution of atmosphere, a shift in emphasis that was in turn accompanied by increasing autonomy on the part of the painting.

Antonello da Messina
Portrait of a Young Man, 1474
Oil on poplar, 32 x 26 cm
Berlin, Staatliche Museen zu
Berlin – Preussischer Kulturbesitz,
Gemäldegalerie

Page 88:
Giovanni Antonio Boltraffio (?)
and Leonardo (?)
Portrait of a Musician, c. 1485
Tempera and oil on wood (walnut?),
44.7 x 32 cm
Milan, Pinacoteca Ambrosiana,
Inv. 99

Page 89:
Portrait of an Unknown
Woman (La Belle Ferronière),
c. 1490–1495
Oil on walnut, 63 x 45 cm
Paris, Musée du Louvre, Inv. 778

I expected to see little more than such designs in anatomy as might be useful to a painter in his own profession. But I saw, and indeed with astonishment, that Leonardo had been a general and a deep student. When I consider what pains he has taken upon every part of the body, the superiority of his universal genius, his particular excellence in mechanics and hydraulics, and the attention with which such a man would examine and see objects which he was to draw, I am fully persuaded that Leonardo was the best anatomist at that time in the world.

WILLIAM HUNTER, 1784

V The artist and "science"

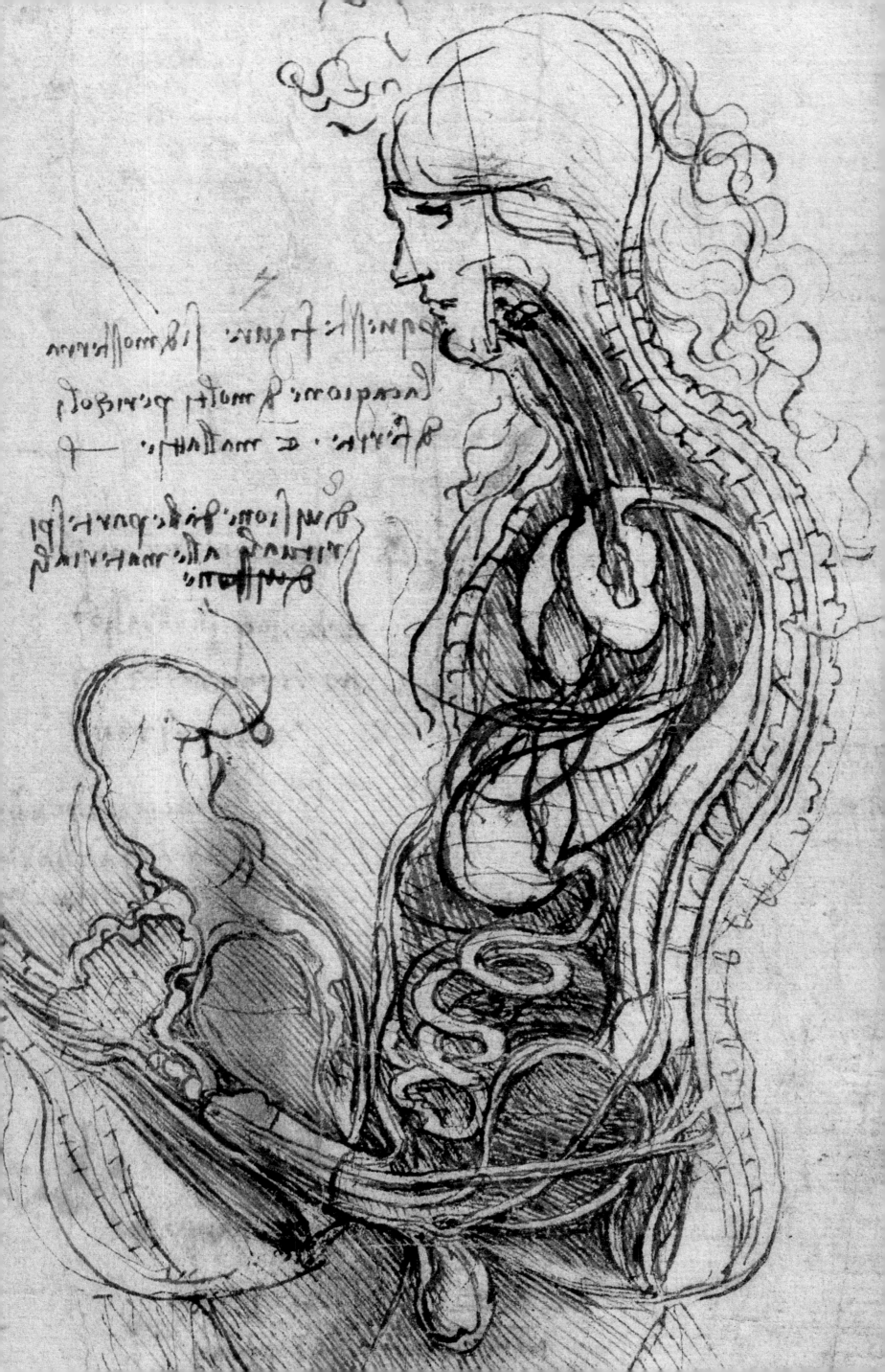

Aristotle (384–322 BC) opens his *Metaphysics* with the observation that all men by nature desire to have knowledge, and hereby stresses the importance of empirical observation. Leonardo da Vinci may be seen as the prototype of such a man, thirsty for knowledge and understanding gained through sensory experience. Leonardo adopts the same dictum in his own writings at the latest around 1490, having assimilated Aristotle's thought via his reading of Dante's (1265–1321) *Convivio* (1306/08; RLW § 10). In a poetic vision that comes closer to Plato's (427–347 BC) cave allegory (*Politeia*, 7.1–3) than to Aristotle, the artist describes his yearning for knowledge thus: "Unable to resist my eager desire and wanting to see the great [wealth] of the various and strange shapes made by formative nature, and having wandered some distance among gloomy rocks, I came to the entrance of a great cavern, in front of which I stood some time, astonished and unaware of such a thing. Bending my back into an arch I rested my left hand on my knee and held my right hand over my down-cast and contracted eyebrows: often bending first one way and then the other, to see whether I could discover anything inside, and this being forbidden by the deep darkness within, and after having remained there some time, two contrary emotions arose in me, fear and desire – fear of the threatening dark cavern, desire to see whether there were any marvellous things within it…" (RLW § 1339).

If Leonardo's thirst for knowledge and discovery was still held in check in this vision by his fear of the threatening unknown, by the end of the 1480s at the latest he had thrown himself with unbridled enthusiasm into the study of a wide range of fields. While working on the preparations for the Sforza monument, he also embarked on more in-depth studies into the proportions of the human body, anatomy and physiology. These studies, which Leonardo's contemporaries frequently dismissed as the artistically unproductive whims of a restless mind, have been acknowledged since the 19th century as the forerunners of an empirical science based on the accurate observation of natural phenomena. In his studies of the human body, for example, and above all in his direct visual translation of his findings and insights, the artist was undoubtedly many generations ahead of his contemporaries. This is true not only of the anatomical studies, which he commenced largely around 1489 and which he intensified at the start of the 1500s, but also of Leonardo's study of the proportions of the human body. In a note made in one of his manuscripts, the artist dates the start of these studies to April 1489 (RLW § 1370).

That same year, or not long afterwards, he began compiling a systematic record of the measurements of a number of young men, two of whom are even identified by name as Trezzo and Caravaggio. He proceeded to record their measurements – from the tips of the toes to the top of their heads – in notes and sketches (ill. p. 93, 95). During virtually exactly the same period he was also taking measurements of the horses owned by his patron Ludovico il Moro. After what must have been months of taking measurements, therefore, Leonardo arrived at an almost complete overview of human proportions, at which point he then started to look at the proportions of sitting and kneeling figures. Finally, he compared the results of his anthropometric studies – i.e. studies involving the systematic measuring of the proportions of the human body – with the only investigation of human proportions to survive from antiquity, namely the *Vitruvian Man*.

Vitruvius (c. 80–c. 20 BC), an only moderately successful architect and engineer during the days of the Roman Empire, wrote a treatise on architecture that included in its third volume a description of the complete measurements of the human body. These led him to conclude that a man with legs and arms outstretched could be inscribed within the perfect geometric figures of the circle and the square alike. These two figures are usually referred to as the *homo ad circulum* and the *homo ad quadratum*, and also as the *Vitruvian Man*. According to Vitruvius's theory, the centre of the human body as inscribed within the square and circle coincided with the navel. Vitruvius's findings

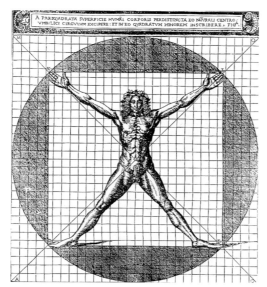

Page 91:
Detail of **The Sexual Act in Vertical Section**, *c.* 1490
Pen and brown ink,
276 x 204 mm
Windsor Castle, Royal Library
(RL 19097 v)

Cesare Cesariano
Vitruvian Man, 1521
From Commentary on Vitruvius,
fol. 50r

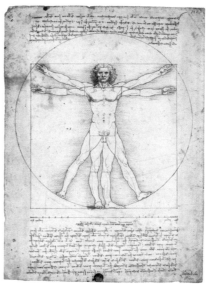

The Proportions of the Human Figure (after Vitruvius), *c.* 1490
Pen, ink and watercolour over metalpoint, 344 x 245 mm
Venice, Gallerie dell'Accademia,
Inv. 228

were taken up again during the Renaissance and in subsequent epochs and illustrated with widely differing results. Best known is the drawing by Leonardo (ill. p. 92); rather more notorious is the later woodcut by the Milanese surveyor Cesare Cesariano (1483–1543), showing a figure who not only has a noteworthy erection but also enormous hands and strikingly long feet (ill. p. 92). Like several authors before and after him, Cesariano interpreted Vitruvius's description from the point of view of the geometry of medieval architecture and related the two figures, circle and square, directly to each other, i.e. the square is exactly contained within the circle. In order for the figure to fit inside this geometric construction, however, it has to stretch out considerably – hence the huge hands and elongated feet. Leonardo, by contrast, did not orient himself towards the geometric relationship between the circle and the square, and in his drawing these two geometric figures are not forcibly related. Rather, he corrected inconsistencies in Vitruvius's proportions on the basis of his own measurements, drawing on the proportions of the human body that he had established by first-hand, empirical observation. Thus the hands and feet in Leonardo's diagram revert to their appropriate size. Only the centre of the *homo ad circulum* now coincides with the navel, whereas the centre of the *homo ad quadratum* is located just above the genitals. By measuring man accurately anew, Leonardo succeeded in moving past the canon of human proportions established in antiquity. His drawing thereby marks a triumph of empiricism over the widely held faith in the authority of classical authors. Furthermore, in his famous, revised drawing of the *Vitruvian Man*, Leonardo created what remains even today the definitive visual statement of the proportions of the human figure.

The theory of proportion was naturally no invention of Leonardo's. The sculptors of antiquity and the artist workshops of the Middle Ages had all employed certain systems of measurement that, if adhered to more or less accurately, would guarantee a satisfactory rendition of the human figure in sculpture and painting. By the second half of the 15th

century, a detailed knowledge of human proportions had already become standard amongst the leading artists of the day, as seen in the case of Antonio (1431/32–1498) and Piero del Pollaiuolo (1443–1496), whose works are clearly based on an intensive study of the measurements of the human body. On the theoretical front, the humanist Leon Battista Alberti (1404–1472) had already developed a canon of proportion in his *De statua*, written before the middle of the century. These earlier efforts by artists and theoreticians, however, fell far short of the standard and accuracy of Leonardo's own studies. Leonardo's anthropometry in turn went far beyond the requirements of normal artistic practice.

Leonardo's interest in an anthropometry of mathematical precision was in part connected with the high regard in which the exact sciences, and with them measurement and geometry, were at that time held. Comparable efforts to establish a "scientific" basis for the fine arts could be found as far back as antiquity: through the rationality of measurement, art too could approach the *logos* and thus a more highly regarded sphere of human activity (Philostratus the Lemnian, *Eikones*, I.I). The artists and theoreticians of the Quattrocento formed part of the same tradition when they tried to confer the higher status of exact science upon art. Thus Alberti sought to establish a "scientific" foundation for art in the first two books of his treatise *De pictura* of 1435. Other authors, such as the mathematician Luca Pacioli (c. 1445–1514) in the dedication to his *Summa de arithmetica, geometria, proportioni et proportionalita* of 1494, honoured the efforts of artists to attain mathematical exactitude in painting by expressly extolling the merits of painters who used dividers and rulers, geometry, arithmetic and perspective. In his commentary on Vitruvius (fol. 46v) of 1521, Cesare Cesariano also stresses that the study of the exact measurements and symmetries of classical buildings leads to fame and social recognition. Leonardo himself argues for the application of mathematical procedures to painting: number and measurement, synonymous with arithmetic and geometry, guarantee a greater degree of certainty and provide the true basis of

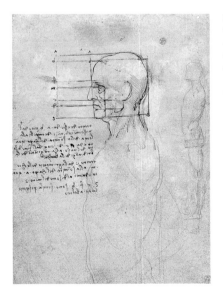

Study of the Proportions of the Head and Face, *c.* 1489/90
Pen and dark brown ink over metalpoint on blue prepared paper, 213 x 153 mm
Windsor Castle, Royal Library
(RL 12601)

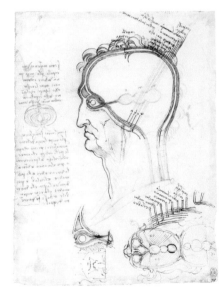

Anatomical Study of the Layers of the Brain and Scalp, *c.* 1490–1493
Pen, two shades of brown ink and red chalk, 203 x 152 mm
Windsor Castle, Royal Library
(RL 12603r)

painting (McM 33). The ennoblement of painting through arithmetic and geometry was still being recommended even in the 16th century. When Leonardo started taking accurate measurements of the human body in 1489, he was driven by the same idea that artistic activities could be elevated to a new status by their marriage with the exact sciences. It would appear that Leonardo's anthropometry was not without effect, for in his ode on the Sforza monument, the poet Baldassare Taccone expressly lauds his artist colleague as a "geometer" (cf. Ch. IV), a term that in 15th-century usage also implied someone with expertise in the field of surveying.

Leonardo's anthropometry and other efforts to provide art with a "scientific" grounding began in earnest only after his arrival in Milan, and in particular towards the end of the 1480s. Leonardo's own career had started in Andrea del Verrocchio's workshop not with a "scientific" training, however, but with a practical apprenticeship. Leonardo acknowledged this practical background when he described himself as "not a man of letters" (*uomo senza lettere*; RLW § 10), in other words as an uneducated man who had not been schooled in the liberal arts. The altogether seven liberal arts had formed the basis of higher education since late antiquity, and were divided into the *trivium* (grammar, logic and rhetoric) and *quadrivium* (geometry, astronomy, arithmetic and music). Not until the late 1480s in Milan did Leonardo begin devoting a significant proportion of his time to studying the traditional branches of science, for example geometry and Latin grammar, in which he was largely self-taught.

In order to understand why Leonardo should want to further his education, it is necessary to be clear about the social status of fine art in the 15th century. Amongst the literati of the Quattrocento, fine art was seen almost without exception not as a liberal art but as an *ars mechanica*, an art that was tied to handicraft. Even by the start of the 16th century painting was still not considered a liberal art and was frequently ranked lower than poetry. In view of this situation, it is no

surprise that Leonardo should have been anxious to establish his reputation in Milan with the help of theoretical and "scientific" studies. At a more personal level, of course, he thereby sought to compete with the men of letters held in higher esteem than himself at the Sforza court.

Indicative of this rivalry were the problems and polemics that arose out of the unrealized project for the equestrian monument to Francesco Sforza. The earliest documented reference to Leonardo's work on the monument is found in a letter of 22 July 1489, which reveals that the important commission was in immediate danger of being given to another sculptor, since Ludovico Sforza had apparently come to the conclusion that Leonardo wasn't up to the job (cf. Ch. IV). When the Milan literati also seized upon the monument as a target for their criticism, Leonardo must have felt his role as a fine artist challenged yet again. July 1489 namely saw the translation into Italian of Giovanni Simonetta's *De gestis Francisci Sphortiae*, a eulogy to Francesco Sforza. The dedication to this Italian edition was written by Francesco Puteolano, who used the occasion to stress the superiority of literary creations over works of fine art. Puteolano expressly pointed out that the memory of great rulers and generals of the past, such as Alexander the Great and Julius Caesar, had been preserved not by monumental works of art but thanks to writers and historians. Small books had guaranteed these men more enduring protection from oblivion than monuments created from the most expensive materials. A ruler was not preserved in the *memoria* of posterity by statues and pictures, which as a rule rapidly deteriorated or were even destroyed and which attracted only criticism – thus Puteolano in his long-winded preface. Possibly as a reaction both to this line of argument and the threat of losing the commission for the equestrian monument to another artist (cf. Ch. IV), in August 1489 Leonardo asked the humanist Piattino Piatti to compose some poems in praise of the work still to be completed. Perhaps he hoped to be able to counter Puteolano's polemics with Piatti's poetry.

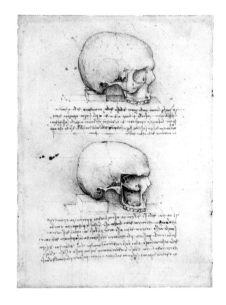

Anatomical Study of the Human Skull in Side View, showing the Eye Sockets and Maxillary Sinus, 1489
Pen and brown ink over black pencil, 188 x 134 mm
Windsor Castle, Royal Library
(RL 19057v)

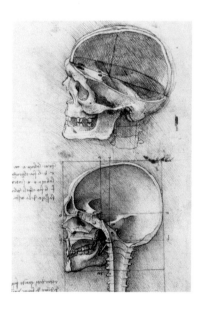

Anatomical Studies of the Human Skull: Sagittal Section in Side View, 1489
Pen and two shades of brown ink over black chalk, 188 x 134 mm
Windsor Castle, Royal Library
(RL 19057r)

Puteolano's remarks unmistakably express an open rivalry between the artists and writers at the Milan court. His comparison, for example, of the eternal *memoria* bequeathed by literary works with the less enduring testament of fragile works of art could not be clearer. Nor is it possible to overlook his allusion to the plans to cast the monumental equestrian statue of Francesco Sforza in costly bronze. In 1489, therefore, both the imminent threat of losing this commission and the doubts cast on the efficacy of fine art by the writers at the Milanese court cast a radical question mark over Leonardo's social status as an artist. It is probably no coincidence that Leonardo should, at this point in time, intensify his researches into proportion and other spheres of knowledge in which he hoped to make a name for himself both as a scientist and an artist. This same period lastly also provided the stimulus for the *Paragone*, the comparison of the arts conducted by Leonardo at the start of his treatise on painting. The fierce dispute being conducted in polemical form between the writers and the artists attached to the Milan court, in which each sought to prove their métier to be superior to that of their opponents, reached an initial climax around 1492 – precisely the period during which Leonardo composed the introduction to his *Trattato di pittura*, in which he takes issue with the poets and writers who had inveighed against the enduring value of fine art. Writing with extraordinary vehemence, Leonardo compares them with "beasts" (RLW § 11/MK 2) and argues against the classification of fine art as one of the lower "artes mecanicae" (RLW, *Paragone*, 9–12, and TPL 19). It is in the light of all these factors, therefore, that Leonardo's intensive efforts to establish a "scientific" grounding for the fine arts must be understood.

Alongside his investigations into the proportions of the human figure, Leonardo ventured even further into the realms of "science" with the anatomical and physiological studies on which he also embarked in grand style towards the end of the 1480s. These years, for example, saw him studying the dimensions of the human skull as well as the different "ventricles" of the brain, even if he thereby allowed himself to be guided in essence by the incorrect but nevertheless widespread theories propounded in antiquity and the Middle Ages. Thus Leonardo accepted the notion of the so-called *senso comune* – literally "common sense", but in those days thought of as the central switchboard of the brain (see below) – and in line with contemporary thinking assigned it a specific location within the brain. Explanatory notes accompanying one of his drawings (Cat. ill. p. 95) make this location clear: "Where the line *a–m* is intersected by the line *c–b*, there will be the confluence of all the senses, and where the line *r–n* is intersected by the line *h–f*, there the fulcrum of the cranium is located at one third up from the base line of the head." Leonardo was thus attempting to apply the principles of anthropometry to the inside of the skull, something yet to be measured with any empirical accuracy. Just as it was possible to determine the measurements of the visible outer parts of the body, so, too, the location inside the body of such an important organ as the *senso comune* was calculated with mathematical precision.

As well as plotting the exact position of the "common sense", Leonardo also identified the location of the other functions of the brain. In a drawing showing vertical and horizontal sections of the human head (ill. p. 93), he takes up traditional medieval notions of the different compartments of the human brain, which he envisages as three chambers the size of nutshells arranged one behind the other. The first of these three chambers contains the *imprensiva*, where sense impressions are received, the second the *senso comune*, and third the *memoria* or memory. An even more striking anatomical misapprehension that Leonardo took over from antiquity and the Middle Ages is evident in his so-called coitus drawings.

In his representation of sexual intercourse, Leonardo draws upon contemporary thinking and the physiology enshrined in the *Corpus Hippocraticum* in depicting the ways in which the internal organs of the human body interconnect. Thus a tube-like duct leads from the

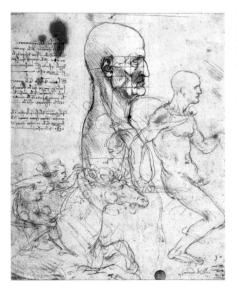

Torso of a Man in Profile, the Head Squared for Proportion, and Two Horsemen, *c.* 1490 and *c.* 1504
Pen and ink and red chalk over metalpoint, 280 x 222 mm
Venice, Gallerie dell 'Accademia, Inv. 236 r

Page 96:
Jacques Daliwe
Character Heads (Christ and two Apostles?), *c.* 1400
Silverpoint on brownish prepared paper, 88 x 129 mm
Berlin, Staatsbibliothek zu Berlin – Preussischer Kulturbesitz, Handschriftenabteilung, Libr. pict. A 74, fol. Va

Jacques Daliwe
Character Heads (Susanna and the Elders), *c.* 1400
Silverpoint (?) on brownish prepared paper, 88 x 129 mm
Berlin, Staatsbibliothek zu Berlin – Preussischer Kulturbesitz, Handschriftenabteilung, Libr. pict. A 74, fol. VIb

Page 97:
Character Head of an Older Man and Sketch of a Lion's Head, *c.* 1505–1510
Red chalk with white heightening on pink prepared paper, 183 x 136 mm
Windsor Castle, Royal Library (RL 12502)

woman's breasts to her womb, while the male organ is directly linked not only to the testicles but also to the lungs and the spinal cord, and hence to the brain. The sketches at the bottom of the sheet, showing a cross section and a longitudinal section of the penis, accordingly portray two channels, the lower for the sperm from the testes and the upper for the spiritual powers transported from the brain along the spinal cord. In his later anatomical drawings, which were based on extensive studies of dissected corpses, Leonardo increasingly questioned these antiquated notions of the human anatomy and how it functions.

Leonardo's conviction that the inner organs of the human being were closely interconnected reflects a highly complex understanding of human nature. The two channels in the penis, for example, illustrate the view that there were two ingredients necessary for procreation: in addition to sperm, a spiritual substance was also required. This spiritual substance, which ultimately came from the very seat of the soul, was thought to carry higher intellectual and spiritual qualities, while the sperm from the testicles, with its own specific make-up, was responsible for baser urges, although also for such properties as courage in battle. Similar notions of the effect and function of bodily substances also informed Leonardo's thinking on tears, which he believed came directly from the heart as the seat of all feeling (RL 19057v).

In order to appreciate the full significance of the physiological notions encountered so far, we must take a closer look at just how Leonardo thought the brain, and in particular the *senso comune*, actually worked. At the heart of this physiology, which presupposes that the processes of the soul exert a direct mechanical influence upon the body and its functions, lie Leonardo's views on the functioning of the brain (ill. p. 93). To Leonardo's understanding, the things perceived by the five senses are sent first to the *imprensiva*, which is no more than a temporary holding centre. The impressions received here are then transferred to the *senso comune* for correlation and evaluation, before finally

being stored in the *memoria*, where they "are more or less retained according to the importance or force of the impression" (RLW § 836).

To Leonardo's way of thinking, the "common sense" is also responsible for the physical expression of mental states, for on the one hand it is the seat of the soul, and on the other it holds sway over the body's means of expression, such as gesture and mien, through the influence it is able to exert on muscles, sinews, tendons and nerves (RLW § 838). The commands issuing from the *senso comune* are thereby conveyed to the organs that are to execute them by means of a vehicle termed a "spirit" (*spirito*). The spirit itself is an incorporeal quality that cannot express itself without a body and hence needs nerves and muscles to produce movements in an animate being (RLW § 859, 1212, 1214).

Leonardo's reflections on the direct links between the spirit and the external features of the body also find their way into his studies of human physiognomy, which similarly presuppose an immediate connection between cause and effect. This immediacy was something the artist sought to illustrate in his countless character heads and caricatures. These drawings – often more grotesque than realistic, and frequently juxtaposing a number of different facial types (ill. p. 98) – express the idea that the human face is a direct reflection of an individual's underlying character and feelings in that moment. According to this view, a man whose face resembles that of a lion in all probability shares the characteristics of the same animal. Leonardo takes up this physiognomic cliché in one of his studies, in which he portrays a man with leonine features wearing a lion-skin flung across his shoulder, the lion's head clearly visible (ill. p. 97). The same idea also underlies Leonardo's famous drawing of five grotesque heads (ill. p. 98): an old man seen in profile is surrounded by four other men, whose powerfully expressive features reveal widely differing and, by implication, negative characteristics. They seem to be mocking the man in the centre, who stoically endures their jeering – his own face

38.

undistorted but nevertheless deeply lined and etched by the hand of fate. Such assemblies of different faces and characters were also a feature of pattern drawings of the type that have come down to us from workshops north of the Alps. Amongst sheets of character heads by Jacques Daliwe (active *c.* 1380–1416), for example, we find *Susanna and the Elders* depicted in a similar fashion (ill. p. 96).

With his studies into the proportions, the anatomy and the physiology of the human body, Leonardo had far from exhausted the spectrum of his interests. Again probably from the end of the 1480s onwards, he also devoted himself to other projects, which had absolutely nothing to do with art. These included not just the war machines encountered earlier (cf. Ch. IV and ill. p. 199), but also designs for flying machines and studies of bird flight. The question of whether Leonardo could ever have got off the ground in any of these devices is of little interest. The artist was probably fully aware of the problems any such attempt would have entailed, for the material weight of some of his machines was alone sufficient to keep them firmly on the ground. He nevertheless returned repeatedly to studies of bird flight, the aerodynamics of flying and the construction of wings. Curiosity and imagination clearly spurred him to execute studies and designs that went far beyond the technological capabilities of his own day. Such was Leonardo's perseverance that one might speak, in his case, of a triumph of "scientific" curiosity over the prospects of practical success. These studies are also indirect evidence of a certain, albeit still modest, prosperity, since Leonardo clearly had the time and financial means to explore areas of knowledge that were more likely to entail costs than to bring money in.

On the basis of what payments Leonardo accumulated his modest savings in the 1490s is not altogether clear, since surviving records are both incomplete and contradictory. Thus Luca Pacioli claims in his *Divina proportione* that Leonardo received only a regular salary as court artist as from 1496 (!), although this does not necessarily mean that the artist was better paid from this point onwards than he had been in previous years. Leonardo's income certainly fluctuated widely, ranging – it is estimated – between 50 and over 100 ducats a year. Nor were artists working for a court always paid regularly in cash; they were occasionally presented with gifts instead. The pros and cons of such a system of remuneration, which depended directly upon the humour and good-

will of the prince concerned, were experienced by Leonardo at first hand. In a lengthy draft of a letter written in 1495/96, he complains about the fact that he still has not been paid: for a period of 36 months he has received only 50 ducats (200 lire), with which it has barely been possible to maintain six people. His salary for two years is still outstanding, and he has been forced to pay for expensive assistants out of his own pocket. In another such draft, he again requests the *premio del mio servizio*, the "reward of my service" (RLW § 1344–1345).

From all appearances, it would seem that during this period – roughly the years 1494 to 1496 – neither the annual salary due to the artist and his workshop, nor individual fees relating to particular projects, were paid regularly or in full. This is confirmed by Leonardo's private accounts, as far as they can be reconstructed. By 1492 the artist had accumulated around 200 ducats (811 lire) and by 1493 had boosted his reserves to 300 ducats – an increase of 50 per cent. This percentage growth was not matched over the following years, however. Thus although Leonardo's cash savings totalled 600 ducats (2400 lire) by 1499, this actually translates into a lower annual growth rate and is possibly a clue that Ludovico Sforza had been feeling less generous towards him. In the spring of 1499, in fact, Ludovico expressly remarked that he had not paid Leonardo enough and that he intended to remunerate him better in future. That same spring he made the artist a gift of a vineyard just outside Milan, whose market value a few years later was taxed at 1100 *lire imperiali*, an amount three or four times higher than the annual salary of a senior official or a university professor. If Leonardo complained about being badly paid, he was still better off than most. Without a relatively solid financial basis, he could not have afforded to keep going without payment, nor would he have had time to spare for his "scientific" studies. Even if it was often late in being paid, it was the income he earned from his many activities as court artist that made it possible for Leonardo to strive towards the universal knowledge for which he would subsequently become famous.

Five Grotesque Heads, *c.* 1490
Pen and ink, 261 x 206 mm
Windsor Castle, Royal Library
(RL 12495r)

Grotesque Portrait Study of a Man, *c.* 1500–1505
Black chalk, reworked by foreign hand (pricked), 390 x 280 mm
Oxford, Governing Body, Christ Church, Inv. JBS 19

Page 99:
Study with Hoist for a Cannon in an Ordnance Foundry, *c.* 1487
Pen and ink on brownish prepared paper, 250 x 183 mm
Windsor Castle, Royal Library
(RL 12647r)

It had a melancholy and delicate palette, rich in shadows, without éclat in the bright colours, and triumphing in the chiaroscuro which, had it not existed, would have had to have been invented for such a subject [the "Last Supper"].

HENRI STENDHAL, 1817

VI From the *Last Supper* to the fall of Ludovico Sforza 1495–1499

Leonardo's reputation in Milan was firmly cemented by the portraits that he painted for the court and by his work on the equestrian monument to Francesco Sforza. It was in his capacity as court artist that he also created undoubtedly the most famous work of his first Milanese period, the *Last Supper* (Cat. XVII/ill. pp. 104/105). Probably commissioned by Ludovico Sforza, the painting was executed between 1495 and 1497 in the refectory of the monastery Santa Maria delle Grazie. None other of Leonardo's works attracted such immediate and rhapsodic praise from his contemporaries as his *Last Supper*. Amongst the first to comment on it was Leonardo's friend Luca Pacioli, who had followed its progress throughout and who wrote an enthusiastic description of it immediately after its completion. Above all, he praised the painting's fidelity to life: it was "not possible to imagine the apostles more agitated upon hearing the voice of unfailing truth, when Jesus said: 'One of you shall betray me'. In their poses and their expressions, they seem to be speaking one to another and this one to that with vigorous astonishment and dismay, as so worthily composed by the skilful hand of our Leonardo." Antonio de Beatis was no less impressed when he visited the Dominican refectory in December 1517, and described the painting as follows: "It is most excellent, although it is beginning to deteriorate – I don't know whether because of the damp in the wall or because of some other inadvertence. The persons in this Last Supper are portraits painted from life of several people at court and of Milanese citizens of the day, in life size. You can also see a sacristy very rich in brocade paraments, similarly donated by the said Ludovico."

The fascination exerted by the *Last Supper* from a very early stage is also documented some ten years later by Paolo Giovio (1483–1552), who – after complaining about Leonardo's "scientific" studies, which had kept him away from painting – goes on to write: "Greatly admired in Milan, nevertheless, is a wall-painting of Christ dining with his disciples. King Louis of France is said to have been so taken with this work that, contemplating it with profound emotion, he asked those around him whether it was possible to remove it from the wall and take it back to France, even if it meant destroying the famous refectory." These early descriptions of Leonardo's wall-painting raise two of the themes that, over the following centuries, would dominate the discussion of the *Last Supper*, namely the rapid deterioration of the work, which was executed in a not very durable tempera technique, and the remarkably varied and life-like poses and gestures of Christ's disciples.

Known the world over in countless copies, reworkings and reproductions (ill. p. 110), Leonardo's *Last Supper* remains the most famous version of its subject. Like the Florentine artists before him, Leonardo portrays the Last Supper in a stage-like setting constructed according to the rules of centralized perspective. The orthogonal lines thereby converge in Christ's head, emphasizing the Saviour's central position within the scene. Leonardo concentrates his composition upon the moment when Jesus sits down with his disciples and declares: "Verily I say unto you, that one of you shall betray me" (*Amen dico vobis, quia unus vestrum me traditurus est;* Matthew 26:21). The shock and horror with which this announcement is greeted by virtually all the disciples are expressed in a wide range of gestures and reactions: at the far left end of the table, Bartholomew rises from his chair in indignation, while beside him James the Younger and Andrew raise their hands in astonishment. Peter has also partly risen from his chair and is looking angrily towards the centre of the picture. In front of him is the traitor Judas, recoiling in shock and with his right hand clutching the pouch containing the money he has been paid to betray Christ. For the first time in the history of post-medieval Last Suppers, Judas is sitting not in front of the table, but behind it. He thereby appears immediately next to John, whose reaction is somewhat muted (he does not yet know he is sitting next to the traitor) and who casts his gaze downwards, almost contemplatively, with folded hands.

Page 101:
Detail of **The Last Supper**,
c. 1495–1497
(ill. pp. 104/105)

Unknown artist
The Last Supper, 1476
*Woodcut, 254 x 352 mm
Milan, Raccolta Vinciana*

Photo of the north wall of the
Refectory
Milan, Santa Maria delle Grazie

Comparatively motionless in the centre of the composition, framed by the opening behind him, sits Jesus himself. He is flanked on his other side by two more groups of three disciples: Thomas, James the Elder and Philip, followed further right by Matthew, Thaddaeus and Simon.

Leonardo's *Last Supper* is exceptional in several respects. It is one of only a handful of paintings executed in Lombardy between 1430 and 1499 that are located in a refectory and that at the same time clearly portray the moment when Jesus announces his impending betrayal. In contrast to similar works by his immediate contemporaries, Leonardo imbues the scene with life both by clustering the twelve apostles into four distinct groups and by endowing his figures with precisely calculated gestures and expressions. Last Suppers by other artists from the same period reveal none of the dramatic intensity of Leonardo's scene (ill. p. 102). Sketches, studies and preparatory drawings relating directly to the final composition, as well as eye-witness reports, all confirm the fact that the artist went to extraordinary lengths to achieve a particularly expressive range of gestures and facial expressions. His efforts were clearly so unusual and so widely reported amongst his contemporaries that Giovanbattista Giraldi (1504–1573) still writes about them decades later: "Whenever Leonardo wanted to paint a figure, he first thought about [that person's] qualities and nature, i.e. about whether they were noble or common, cheerful or stern, troubled or happy, old or young, angry or calm, good or bad. And when he had established their character, he went to where he knew people of this kind would be gathered, and diligently observed their faces, their mannerisms, their dress and the movements of their bodies. And when he had found something that was suitable for his purposes, he recorded it with a pen in a notebook that he always wore on his belt. And when he had done this many, many times and had gathered what seemed to be enough for his painting, he started to fashion it, and he made it succeed marvellously. Even assuming this is what he did in all his works, he did so with par-

ticular diligence in the picture that he painted in Milan in the monastery of the Friars Preacher, in which our Saviour is shown seated at table with his disciples."

Giraldi's detailed description is fully confirmed by Leonardo's writings. In the treatise on painting, which he commenced around 1490, Leonardo wrote that, when out for a walk, a painter should observe the poses and faces of the people around him and jot them down in a notebook. The motifs of movement and expression captured in this way would lead on to rough compositions (*componimento inculto*), which could then be developed and perfected (TPL 290, 173, 179, 189). That these recommendations were rooted in Leonardo's own practice is suggested by notes he made during the early stages of his work on the *Last Supper*. In a notebook today known as the Codex Forster (RLW § 665–667), he wrote down the names of several people whose hands and faces he wanted to use in the *Last Supper*. In the same manuscript he also describes the very wide-ranging reactions of the disciples to Christ's announcement that he is to be betrayed – the scene, in other words, which he would portray in the final composition.

It is interesting in this context to examine to what extent the descriptions in Leonardo's notebook correspond to the reactions displayed by the disciples in the final painting, executed shortly afterwards. In the following passage, for example, Leonardo explores ideas for two of his figures: "One who was drinking has left his glass in its place and turned his head towards the speaker. Another wrings the fingers of his hands and turns with a frown to his companion" (MK § 579). None of the figures in the final composition in fact appears exactly as described here. Only John, to the left of Christ, has his fingers intertwined and is inclining his head towards the group formed by Judas and Peter, albeit without raising his brows. Further poses outlined in Leonardo's notes similarly bear only a partial resemblance to those adopted by the disciples in the final painting: "Another with hands spread open to show the palms shrugs his shoulders up his ears

Preliminary Sketch for the
Last Supper, c. 1495
Pen and ink, 266 x 215 mm
Windsor Castle, Royal Library
(RL 12542)

Those who put the moustache on Mona Lisa are not attacking it, or art, but Leonardo da Vinci the man. What irritates them is that this man with half a dozen pictures has this great name in history, whereas they, with their large oeuvre, aren't sure.

BARNETT NEWMAN, 1992

VII From Mantua to Venice and back to Florence 1500–1503

Following the fall of Ludovico Sforza, up till then his most important patron, Leonardo went first to Mantua, where Isabella d'Este had established a reputation for herself as a generous if somewhat capricious patron of the arts. It was probably here, in December 1499 or early the next year, that Leonardo produced a cartoon for a portrait of Isabella, who is seen in profile in the tradition of Mantuan court portraiture (Cat. XXI/ill. p. 116). The genealogical portraits of the d'Este family in Mantua, for example, employ the same profile view. The cartoon, to which Isabella also refers in later letters (see below), did not immediately lead to other commissions in Mantua, however, and so Leonardo travelled on to Venice, where he may have been briefly employed as a military engineer.

Although he does not appear to have produced any paintings in the city of canals, the subtle shading in his pictures is said to have influenced Venetian colleagues such as Giorgione – at least according to Giorgio Vasari in his *Life of Giorgione*. Vasari's claim is partially corroborated by a letter from Lorenzo Gusnasco to Isabella d'Este of 13 March 1500, which makes it clear that Leonardo had taken his pictures with him to Venice and had shown them to other people there: "Leonardo is here in Venice, and he has shown me a portrait of Your Highness, which resembles you very closely, is very well done and could not be bettered."

Leonardo must have left Venice fairly quickly and returned to Florence, for on 24 April 1500 he withdrew 50 gold ducats out of the account to which he had transferred the 600 ducats from Milan the previous December. He probably brought back with him the *Burlington House Cartoon* portraying the Virgin and Child with St Anne and the infant St John (Cat. XX/ill. p. 118). The origins of the cartoon, which today hangs in London, are the subject of some controversy. It possibly represents the preparatory design for a painting of St Anne commissioned by Louis XII as a gift for his wife Anne de Bretagne (1477–1514). The final painting was never executed, however, but at least one surviving preliminary sketch (ill. p. 150) and the cartoon itself convey an accurate impression of the overall composition of the proposed picture.

The figures are placed in front of a rocky landscape, Mary sitting sideways on the lap of her mother Anne. The Christ Child seems to be slipping out of her arms and, with his hand raised in a gesture of blessing, is turned towards the infant St John, who is approaching from the right. With this gesture of blessing Leonardo establishes an obvious link with the *Virgin of the Rocks*, in which Jesus and John are also portrayed facing each other. In the gesture of St Anne, who is pointing upwards with her index finger, Leonardo takes up a gesture found

earlier in his *Adoration of the Magi*. Certain parts of the cartoon are considerably more finished than others. While the feet of both women and St Anne's left hand are rendered in little more than outline, the faces are fully modelled and, with their deep shadows and white highlights, already exhibit some of the qualities of a finished oil painting.

In comparison with Leonardo's other compositions, the *Burlington House Cartoon* drew little response from other artists of the day. Of his contemporaries, only Bernardino Luini (*c.* 1480–1532) took over Leonardo's composition in its entirety in his painting of the *Holy Family*, executed in Milan around 1530 (ill. p. 119). He thereby added the figure of Joseph on the right-hand edge of the panel. The possibility cannot be ruled out that Leonardo had also envisaged a Joseph in his painting. Whatever the case, Luini's *Holy Family* provides a general impression of what Leonardo's painting might have looked like had it been finished. It also reveals, even more clearly than the *Burlington House Cartoon* itself, an underlying structure that deviates strongly from Leonardo's previous compositions. Thus the pyramidal, centralized constellation of figures seen in almost all of Leonardo's earlier paintings, such as the *Virgin with the Carnation*, the *Benois Madonna*, the *Portrait of Cecilia Gallerani* and the *Virgin of the Rocks*, is absent from the *Burlington House Cartoon*, whose figures instead betray a lack of overall cohesion. It is not outside the bounds of possibility, in this regard, that Leonardo discarded the *Burlington House Cartoon* precisely because it failed to achieve, in the grouping of its figures, the compositional tautness that distinguished his known works up till then.

According to Giorgio Vasari, Leonardo had another opportunity to produce a cartoon of St Anne not long after his return to Florence. Vasari's report is unreliable on a number of counts, however. He claims, for example, that Leonardo was commissioned to execute a painting of St Anne for the high altar of SS Annunziata, but we know for a fact that a quite different subject had been chosen for this altarpiece. It is more likely that Leonardo executed his cartoon for the Giacomini-Tebalducci family chapel, which was dedicated to St Anne and was located inside the church of SS Annunziata.

It was probably this cartoon that Vasari, although he had never seen it, describes in such astonishing detail: "… finally he did a cartoon showing Our Lady with St Anne and the Infant Christ. This work not only won the astonished admiration of all the artists but when finished for two days it attracted to the room where it was exhibited a crowd of men and women, young and old, who flocked there, as if they were attending a great festival, to gaze in amazement at the marvels he had created. For in the face of Our Lady are seen all the simplicity and

Page 115:
Detail of **Portrait of Lisa del Giocondo (Mona Lisa)**, **1503–1506 and later (1510?)**
(ill. p. 127)

Half-length Portrait of a Young Woman in Profile (Isabella d'Este), *c.* **1499/1500**
Black and red chalk on paper, pricked, 63 x 46 cm
Paris, Musée du Louvre,
Inv. M.I. 753

Page 118:
Burlington House Cartoon (Virgin and Child with St Anne and the Infant St John), 1499–1500 or *c.* 1508 (?)
Charcoal, with white chalk heightening, on brownish paper, mounted on canvas, 141.5 x 106.5 cm (max. dimensions)
London, National Gallery,
Inv. 6337

Leonardo begins with the interior, the mental space, and not with measured outlines, and to finish – if he finishes at all and does not leave the picture incomplete – lays a ghostly body of colour over the true, incorporeal image, quite impossible to describe in material form.

OSWALD SPENGLER, 1917

loveliness and grace that can be conferred on the mother of Christ, since Leonardo wanted to show the humility and modesty appropriate to an image of the Virgin who is overflowing with joy at seeing the beauty of her Son. She is holding him tenderly in her lap, and she lets her pure gaze fall on St John, who is depicted as a little boy playing with a lamb; and this is not without a smile from St Anne, who is supremely joyful as she contemplates the divinity of her earthly progeny."

Whether Vasari is here describing a St Anne composition that has since been lost, or whether he has simply muddled up the descriptions of two different designs, is a question that has yet to be fully clarified. Was he perhaps mixing up a composition such as the *Burlington House Cartoon*, portraying a Virgin and Child with St Anne and including an infant St John, with a cartoon featuring a lamb in place of St John? All we know for certain is that by April 1501 Leonardo had completed a cartoon of the Virgin and Child with St Anne and a lamb, but without an infant St John. This cartoon is mentioned in a letter of 3 April 1501 sent to Isabella d'Este by the Carmelite monk Fra Pietro da Novellara: "Your Most Illustrious, Excellent and Singular Lady, I have just received Your Excellency's letter and will carry out with all speed and diligence that which you instruct me to do. From what I gather, the life that Leonardo leads is haphazard and extremely unpredictable, so that he seems to live only from day to day. Since he came to Florence he has done the drawing of a cartoon. He is portraying a Christ Child of about a year old who is almost slipping out of his Mother's arms to take hold of a lamb, which he then appears to embrace. His Mother, half rising from the lap of St Anne, takes hold of the Child to separate him from the lamb (a sacrificial animal) signifying the Passion. St Anne, rising slightly from her sitting position, appears to want to restrain her daughter from separating the Child from the lamb. She is perhaps intended to represent the Church, which would not have the Passion of Christ impeded. These figures are life-sized but can fit into a small

cartoon because all are either seated or bending over and each one is positioned a little in front of each other and to the left-hand side. This drawing is as yet unfinished. He has done nothing else save for the fact that two of his apprentices are making copies and he puts his hand to one of them from time to time. He is hard at work on geometry and has no time for the brush. I write this only to let Your Excellency know that I have received your letters. I shall carry out Your Excellency's commission and keep Your Excellency informed. I commend myself to Your Excellency and may God keep Her in his grace..." (MK § 669).

Novellara's description may be counted as reliable not just in view of the wealth and accuracy of the details it contains, but also because it tallies with a painting by Brescianino (*c.* 1487–1525), a Sienese artist active in the early 16th century, which is based on Leonardo's cartoon and portrays the Virgin and Child with St Anne and a lamb in a figural group angled towards the left (Cat. XXIIa and b/ill. p. 119, 191). The figures in Brescianino's painting are closely interrelated and the Child is playing busily with the lamb in the bottom left-hand corner. A very similar formal sequence can be seen in Raphael's *Holy Family with a Lamb* of 1507 (ill. p. 119). The young artist had clearly seen Leonardo's cartoon, made an immediate copy of it and then used the composition at a later date as the starting-point for his own painting. In particular the relationship between the Virgin, the Child and the lamb in Raphael's painting reveals a close kinship with the lost work by Leonardo, while the figure of Joseph is based on a somewhat earlier model – Filippino Lippi's *Adoration of the Magi* of 1496 (ill. p. 53), the painting that replaced Leonardo's unfinished altarpiece for San Donato a Scopeto (cf. Ch. II). In both Raphael's painting and Filippino's altarpiece, Joseph is leaning over the group of the mother and child from behind with a staff in his hand. Indeed, not only did Filippino's *Adoration* provide Raphael with the model for Joseph in his *Holy Family with a Lamb*, but it was probably also a starting-point for the constellation of the fig-

Bernardino Luini
Holy Family with St Anne and the Infant St John, *c.* 1530
Oil on wood, 118 x 92 cm
Milan, Pinacoteca Ambrosiana

Raphael
Holy Family with a Lamb,
1507
Oil on wood, 29 x 21 cm
Madrid, Museo Nacional del Prado

Unknown artist, after
Brescianino
Virgin and Child with
St Anne, *c.* 1501 (?)
Oil (?) on wood, 129 x 94 cm
Madrid, Museo Nacional del Prado,
Inv. 505 (899)

of his own choosing and entirely in his own time, Leonardo should not want to work for the Marchioness of Mantua, the most distinguished patroness of the arts in the Renaissance era. Yet during this same period, it has been shown, Leonardo was living on the savings he had transferred to his Florence account before leaving Milan. The artist today known above all as a painter evidently preferred to pursue the "scientific" studies, which brought him in no money and which, indeed, were rather looked down on by his contemporaries. Against this backdrop, it is all the more astonishing that Leonardo should accept, in the spring of 1503, a commission from Francesco del Giocondo (1460–1539) to paint his wife Lisa Gherardini (1479–after 1551?). It is possible that the commission for the *Mona Lisa* (Cat. XXV/ill. p. 127), as the portrait would become known, resulted from personal contacts similar to those that gave rise to other of Leonardo's works, such as the *Portrait of Ginevra de' Benci* and the *Adoration of the Magi*. The Giocondo family belonged to the same social class as Leonardo himself and Ser Piero da Vinci, Leonardo's father, was acquainted with members of Francesco del Giocondo's close circle. In addition, the Giocondo family chapel was located in SS Annunziata in Florence, the same church, in other words, for which Leonardo had begun the cartoon of the Virgin and Child with St Anne at the start of his second Florentine period.

We are relatively well informed about the genesis of the *Mona Lisa*. Lisa del Giocondo, born in 1479, was the daughter of Antonmaria Gherardini. On 5 March 1495 she married Francesco del Giocondo, born in 1460, the son of a wealthy family of Florentine silk merchants. We can assume that, unlike Marchioness Isabella d'Este (see above), a man like Francesco del Giocondo did not commission paintings simply on a whim and regardless of their subject. As a rule, members of the urban middle classes had specific reasons for commissioning works of art, and this is also true of the portrait of the *Mona Lisa*. In the spring of 1503 Francesco del Giocondo had purchased a new house for his young family, while Lisa had given birth to her second son,

Andrea, a few months previously – reason enough, in the Florence of the 15th and 16th centuries, to commission a portrait. In the case of the Giocondo family, moreover, Andrea's safe delivery must have carried particular significance. Levels of infant mortality and death in childbirth were in those days very high, something of which both Francesco and Lisa del Giocondo would have been painfully aware. Francesco had already lost two wives prior to Lisa, on each occasion after about a year of marriage. One of these wives is known to have died shortly after the birth of a child, and it seems likely that both of Francesco's previous wives died either in childbirth or in the weeks immediately following their confinements. Francesco's third wife, Lisa, had evidently survived the birth of her first son Piero (1496), but in 1499 lost a daughter at birth. Childbirth was thus an occasion overshadowed by tragedy for the del Giocondo family. When, in the spring of 1503, some four months after Andrea's birth, mother and son were still doing well, Francesco could allow himself to assume that both would safely survive the happy event. It was this confident that which in all probability prompted Francesco to commission a portrait of his wife to adorn their new home. The portrait of Lisa del Giocondo would never hang in the house for which it was intended, however, since Leonardo did not complete the painting until several years later, probably towards 1510, by which time he was no longer living in Florence.

Leonardo clearly draws in the *Mona Lisa* upon the formal vocabulary of Florentine portraiture of the late 15th century. The half-length figure is turned two-thirds towards the viewer, and a balustrade carried on slender pillars provides the point of transition between the foreground and the background landscape. Formally similarly half-length portraits of young women from the period before 1500 include those by the so-called Master of Santo Spirito and Lorenzo di Credi (ill. p. 132). These in turn look back to earlier Flemish prototypes such as Jan van Eyck's portrait of Isabella of Portugal, now lost (ill. p. 126).

Unknown 17th-century artist
Copy of the Portrait of Isabella of Portugal by Jan van Eyck
Pen drawing, with wash (?)
Location unknown

Unknown artist (Bolognese?)
Virgin and Child
Tempera (?) on wood
Milan, Private Collection, Collezione G.M.N.

Portrait of Lisa del Giocondo (Mona Lisa), 1503–1506 and later (1510?)
Oil on poplar, 77 x 53 cm
Paris, Musée du Louvre, Inv. 779

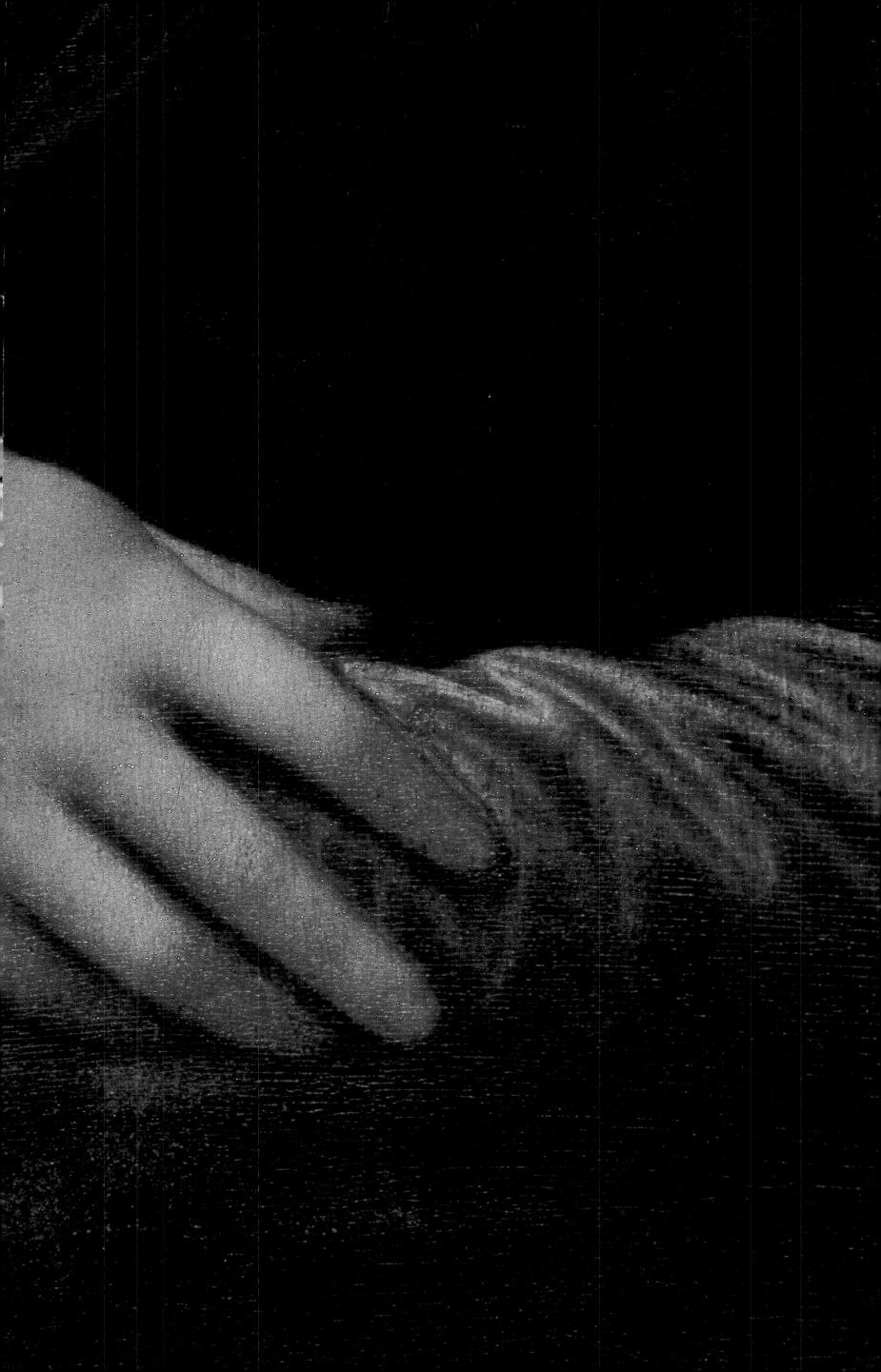

Vinci, however, whose painting expresses a degree of intelligence which has not been equalled, and whose drawing, as the first in Europe to do so, gives us the impression of knowing no obstacle (like that of Chinese and Japanese painters), this Vinci held three of his works to be most important: the equestrian statue of Francesco Sforza, the "Last Supper" and the "Battle of Anghiari."

ANDRÉ MALRAUX, 1951

VIII Leonardo in Florence 1504–1506: Battle paintings and "muscular rhetoric"

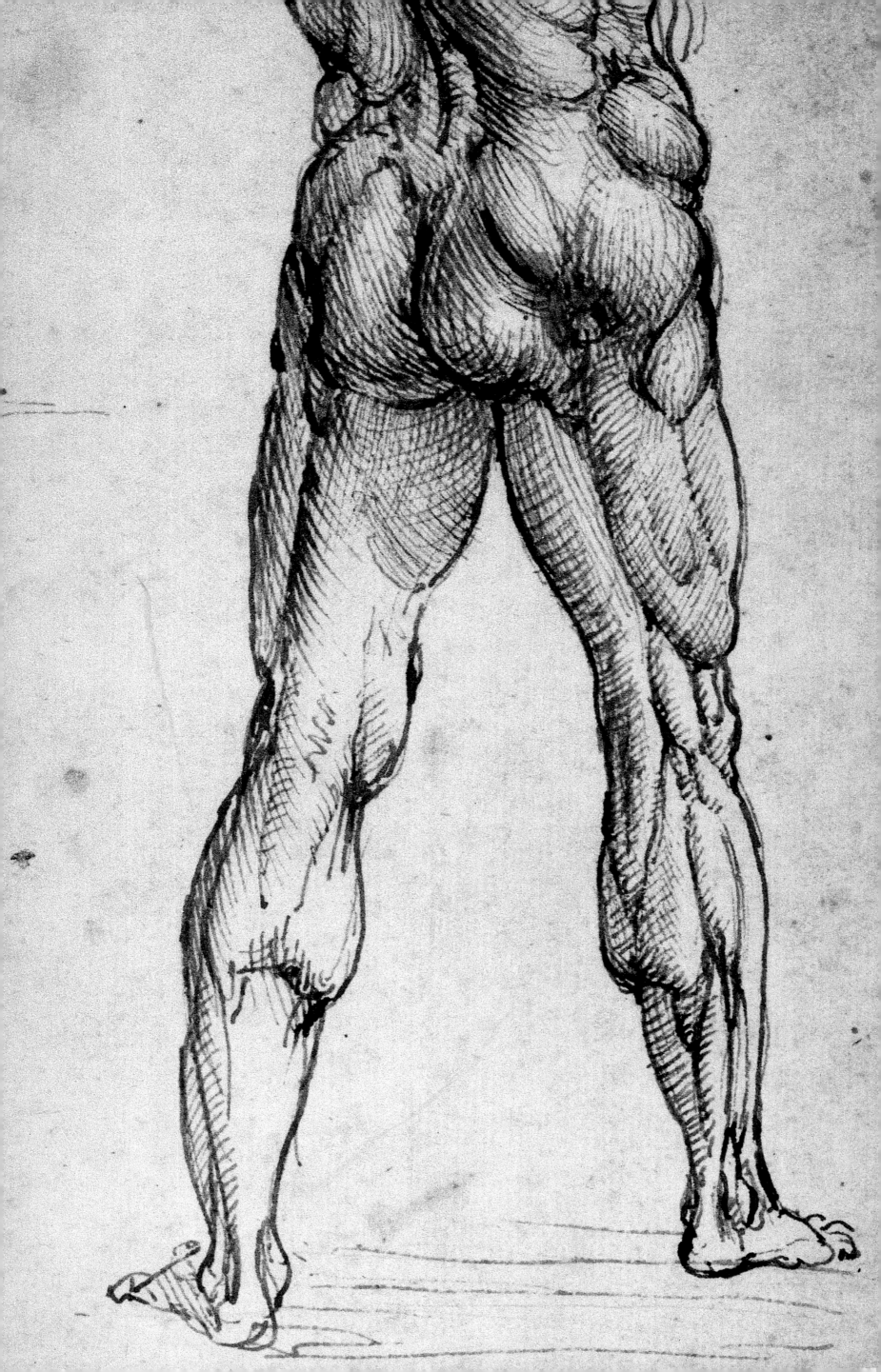

renege on the contract. Should he fail to complete the cartoon within the timeframe agreed, moreover, he will be obliged to hand over what work he has completed, the implication being that the execution of the wall-painting will be entrusted to another artist: "And in the event that the said Leonardo shall not, in the stipulated time, have finished the said cartoon, then the aforesaid Magnifici Signori can compel him by whatever means appropriate to repay all the money received in connection with this work up to the said date and the said Leonardo would be obliged to make over to the said Magnifici Signori as much as had been done of the cartoon, and that within the said time the said Leonardo be obliged to have provided the drawing for the said cartoon."

Since the representatives of the Florentine government were well aware that artists frequently failed to meet their contractual deadlines and that effective sanctions against breaches of contract were often impossible to put in place, in the next section of the document they adopt a milder tone. Thus they grant Leonardo the option, should he exceed the deadline for completing the cartoon, of starting work directly on the wall-painting. "And since it might occur that the said Leonardo will have been able to begin painting on to the wall of the said Sala that part which he had drawn and submitted on the said cartoon, the Magnifici Signori, in that event, would be content to pay him a monthly salary befitting such a painting and as agreed upon with the said Leonardo. And if the said Leonardo thus spends his time painting on the said wall

Unknown artist/Peter Paul Rubens
Copy after Leonardo's Battle
of Anghiari, before 1550 and
c. **1603**
Black chalk, pen, ink, heightened
with white lead, reworked in
watercolour, 452 x 637 mm
Paris, Musée du Louvre

the aforesaid Magnifici Signori will be content to prolong and extend the above-mentioned period during which the said Leonardo is obliged to produce the cartoon in that manner and to whatever length of time as will be agreed by the said Magnifici Signori and the said Leonardo."

Finally, the employers even concede that Leonardo may finish the cartoon if he so wishes, and they pledge that they will not give a fully finished cartoon to another painter to transfer onto the wall: "And since it might also occur that Leonardo within the time in which he has undertaken to produce the cartoon may have no opportunity to paint on the wall but seeks to finish the cartoon, according to his obligation as stated above, then the aforesaid Magnifici Signori agree that

the painting of that particular cartoon shall not be commissioned from anyone else, nor removed from the said Leonardo without his express consent but that the said Leonardo shall be allowed to provide the painting when he is in a position to do so [...]" (MK § 668).

The first half of the agreement thus reveals the employers seeking to impose strict performance targets on the notoriously unreliable Leonardo, while the second half grants him greater room for man œuvre as a paradoxical means of binding him more closely to his obligations. At the end of the day, however, these subtle tactics were all for naught: although Leonardo did indeed start painting on the wall of the Council Chamber, he used an experimental technique that led to the early ruin of the whole. When lucrative commissions from the king of

Aristotele da Sangallo
Battle of Cascina, copy after Michelangelo's cartoon,
c. **1542**
Grisaille, 76.4 x 130.2 cm
Holkham Hall, Collection of the Earl of Leicester

France subsequently beckoned, he left Florence to seek his fortune once again in Milan (cf. Ch. IX).

As in the case of many other documents and contracts from this era, the text cited above tells us nothing about the actual content of the *Battle of Anghiari*. Details of this nature must have been supplied separately, something of which in the present case we have concrete evidence. Thus we know from a sheet in the Codex Atlanticus that Leonardo was provided with a detailed account of the battle of Anghiari (RLW § 669). He made only limited use of this account in his final composition, however. Further evidence that Leonardo may have deviated from his original plans is found in his preparatory sketches (ill. pp. 140, 141). They reveal that the artist had initially envisaged a broad composition incorporating several different events. He appears to have planned various skirmishes between foot soldiers and smaller bands of armed horsemen on either side of the battle for the standard, and on the far right the arrival of a cavalry division (ill. p. 141). In both his cartoon and his final wall-painting, however, Leonardo omitted these previously planned episodes and concentrated exclusively on a single, central battle scene. Only in the physiognomies of the individual riders did he adhere more closely to his preliminary studies (ill. p. 165), whereby two of the soldiers in his drawings retained exactly the same facial features in the final wall-painting.

The surviving copies of the *Battle of Anghiari* (ill. pp. 138) primarily show four horsemen fighting furiously for possession of a standard. The dramatis personae comprise, on the left, Francesco Piccinino and his father Niccolò, the two leaders of the Milanese troops. Their opponents on the right are Piergiampaolo Orsini and Ludovico Scarampo, protagonists of the allied papal and Florentine troops, who were to triumph in the conflict and with whom contemporary viewers would have been able to identify. The physiognomies of the two riders on the left are angry and positively distorted. The features of Niccolò Piccinino, contorted into a loud cry, are impressively captured in a partial copy of the original composition, while the fury written on the face of his son Francesco emerges clearly in copies of the whole. Francesco's brutal grimace is accompanied by a contortion of his upper body, as though his torso were merging into the body of the horse. Man and beast become a single creature, whose uncontrolled rage finds appropriate expression in an unnaturally twisted body.

Contemporary viewers must thereby have been reminded of centaurs, creatures made up of the upper body of a human and the lower body of a four-legged animal. Such creatures are known to have carried negative connotations in the mythographical traditions of the Middle Ages, and in other sources, such as the *Etymologiae* by St Isidore of Seville (*c.* 560–636), they are seen as the prototype of the fighter driven by animal instincts. Francesco's centaur-like figure was undoubtedly intended to invoke the same bestial connotations. The physical fusion of horse and rider, at first sight so strange, also makes reference to Francesco's brutish nature, his angry and martial character, something also mentioned in contemporary sources.

In this context, it is probably no coincidence that in one of the most famous frescoes in a Tuscan government building, Ambrogio Lorenzetti's (active 1319–1348) *Allegory of Bad Government* (1337–1340) in the Palazzo Pubblico in Siena, Fury (*furor*) is portrayed in the shape of a similar creature. The personification of Fury is namely here composed of the lower body of a four-legged animal, a human upper body and the head of a beast (ill. p. 136). This figure may well have sprung to Leonardo's mind when he came to design his own wall-painting, not least because Ambrogio Lorenzetti's frescoes in Siena belonged to the same genre as Leonardo's *Battle of Anghiari*: both formed the decorations for a civic palace.

Less dramatic in their poses are the two protagonists of the Florentine troops and their papal allies. While there is nothing peaceable about their actions, their faces, seen in profile, are far less distorted and their bodies are not contorted. They represent a different, more bal-

Sketch of Galloping Horsemen and Foot Soldiers,
c. 1503/04
Red chalk, 168 x 240 mm
Windsor Castle, Royal Library
(RL 12340r)

Antique cameo:
The Fall of Phaeton
Drawing
Formerly Medici Collection

anced ideal of combat, one that Leonardo's contemporaries evidently found less interesting than the negative embodiment of unbridled bellicosity in their opponents. Thus Vasari concentrates in his own description of the painting above all on Niccolò Piccinino and his son Francesco. He was so impressed by the vindictive rage of the figures that he even muddled up the two warring parties.

Francesco Piccinino is characterized not only by the expression of vicious rage on his face but also by his armour, which clearly reveals several of the attributes of Mars, the god of war. Thus the ram on his chest is the animal symbol of Mars, and the horns of Amon on his head and the ram's fleece on his body are both derived from traditional Mars iconography. The painting thereby alludes to the fact that condottieri such as Niccolò and Francesco Piccinino were considered "children of Mars" and enjoyed a bad reputation; the fact that they sold their services on the battlefield for money made their allegiance ultimately unpredictable. Mars thus stood for an irrational and particularly corrupt form of warfare, quite the opposite of the Florentine ideal of a controlled military operation. In Leonardo's wall-painting, the leaders of the Florentine troops approaching from the right, their faces far less contorted with combative rage, represent the new ideal of warfare being propagated in Florence, namely one employing considered tactical strategy. The helmets of the Florentine soldiers are surmounted in certain copies by a winged dragon, a symbol of circumspection and prudence (*prudentia*; cf. ill. p. 136), and in almost all the rest by the mask of Minerva, the goddess who, according to classical literature, guaranteed prudence in warfare and victory over the rash and thoughtless aggression of Mars. In the portrayal of the central characters, Leonardo's painting thus reveals an antithetical underlying structure, in which Good (Minerva with *prudentia*) is opposed to Evil (Mars with *furor*).

The motif of fighting horsemen was one that had occupied Leonardo even before the *Battle of Anghiari*. It can be found, for exam-

ple, in the background of his *Adoration of the Magi* of 1481/82 (cf. Ch. II). In the 1480s Leonardo also produced drawings of battles between riders and dragons, which derive their dynamism from the confrontation between two opposing forces (ill. p. 142). Similar horse and rider motifs exhibiting a comparable degree of animation would subsequently resurface in Leonardo's designs for the Trivulzio monument of *c.* 1508–1511. In formal terms, however, Leonardo's earlier drawings of battles between dragons and horsemen differ in an important respect from the composition of the battle for the standard. Whereas the opposing parties in the earlier drawings still maintain a minimum of distance between them, in the *Battle of Anghiari* they are in such close contact that even the horses appear to be fighting one another. The decision to bring the horses so close together that they are able to bite each other was probably a later modification of the originally more broadly spaced design. It does not appear in Leonardo's first exploratory sketch for the composition, but only in the second (ill. p. 141). This narrowing of the composition looks back to the *Fall of Phaeton*, a classical motif known in Florence from an antique cameo and including two horses in close contact (ill. p. 140). In addition to its aesthetic appeal, the *Fall of Phaeton* carried a decidedly moral message. The young Phaeton had been granted permission by his father Helios to drive the chariot of the sun for one day. But the adventure ended in tragedy when the inexperienced and overly bold youth lost control of the dangerous team of horses, fell out of the chariot and thereby set the world on fire. The arrogant young man had thus set himself a challenge that exceeded his modest capabilities.

References to the story of Phaeton could also be found in literature, where they implied a moral condemnation of arrogant behaviour. This is the conclusion underlying Ovid's retelling of the story in his *Metamorphoses* (2.19–332) and echoes again in Dante's *Divine Comedy* (Inferno, 17.111) and in Cristoforo Landino's 15th-century commentary on Dante. In view of the subject's pronouncedly moral interpretation by

Study of Horsemen in Combat and Foot Soldiers (sketch for the Battle of Anghiari), 1503
Pen and ink, 101 x 142 mm
Venice, Gallerie dell'Accademia, Inv. 216

[...] in reality theory resides in the intellect, but practice lies in the hands, and this is why Leonardo da Vinci, supremely intelligent, was never satisfied with what he did and only completed a handful of works, often giving as his reason the fact that his hand could not match his mind.

SEBASTIANO SERLIO, 1551

[...] at a stroke, he breaks with the traditional painting of the 15th century; he arrives without errors, without failings, without exaggerations and as if in one bound at this judicious and erudite naturalism, far from servile imitation and an empty, fleeting ideal.

EUGÈNE DELACROIX, 1860

IX Between Florence and Milan 1506–1510

The reasons that prompted Leonardo to break off work on the *Battle of Anghiari* in the spring of 1506, and finally to abandon the painting altogether, were various in nature. Vasari reports of friction between the artist and his employers arising out of the way in which he was paid. Problems to do with Leonardo's unconventional paint medium were another factor, for in the *Battle of Anghiari* – as in the case of the *Last Supper* a few years previously – Leonardo had again decided against executing his mural rapidly *a fresco*. He experimented instead with oil binders with the aim of extending the amount of time his paints were workable on the surface of the wall. Leonardo might also have had personal motives for returning to Milan: in April 1506, just under two years after the death of his father on 7 July 1504, Leonardo's brothers proceeded to cut him out of his father's will, leaving his ties to his family and hence to Florence severely strained. The ongoing dispute over a bonus payment for the second version of the *Virgin of the Rocks* (cf. Ch. III), which had revived itself in 1503, may also have made a trip to Milan necessary. What ultimately caused Leonardo to abandon the *Battle of Anghiari* and leave Florence, however, was probably the fact that a number of other patrons were trying to secure his services and that he was now aware, more than ever before, of his worth as an artist.

Isabella d'Este had been pursuing him for years with requests for a portrait or indeed a painting of any kind. In May 1506 the Marchioness even called in Alessandro Amadori, one of Leonardo's uncles, in the hope of finally achieving the object of her desires, but in vain: the artist had already set his sights even higher. The contacts with the French that he had probably first established in Milan in 1499 (cf. Ch. VI) proved to be the more promising option, for both Charles d'Amboise, the French governor in Milan, and the king of France himself expressed great interest in the work of the Florentine artist. In the hope of securing an appointment with the French court, on 30 May 1506 Leonardo obtained three months' leave from his work on the *Battle of Anghiari*. An agreement regulating this leave of absence thereby stipulated that the artist had to return to Florence in three months' time; should he fail to do so, he would have to pay the not inconsiderable sum of 150 gold ducats. Despite this threat of a fine, the artist did not return to Florence within the appointed time. With the help of the French governor in Milan, he managed to get the deadline extended several times, making it increasingly unlikely that he would ever fulfil his obligations in Florence.

The French king and Charles d'Amboise (d. 1511) were naturally more attractive as patrons than either the Florentine Republic, rocked by crises and in dire economic straits, or Isabella d'Este, Marchioness of Mantua, whose wishes could not compete with the commissions potentially offered by the most powerful monarch in Europe. In their correspondence with the Florentine government, the French for their part conveyed the impression that they were extraordinarily interested in Leonardo and his art. The clearest evidence of this is a letter of 16 December 1506, in which Charles d'Amboise attempts to pacify an enraged Piero Soderini, the Florentine gonfalonier. On 9 October 1506 Soderini had complained bitterly about Leonardo's breach of contract and referred to his unfulfilled obligations. In his reply, Charles d'Amboise adopts a conciliatory tone, promising that the artist will soon be departing for Florence and praising him in the most effusive terms: "The distinguished works which Master Leonardo da Vinci, your fellow Florentine, has left behind in Italy, and in particular in this city [Milan], dispose all who see them to hold him in particular affection, even if they have never met him. And we must confess that we, too, number amongst those who held him dear even before we met him in person. Having had dealings with him and having experienced his talents [*virtute*] for ourselves, however, we saw truly that his name, made famous through painting, still shines less brightly than it deserves in view of his other talents. And we must admit that in the things he produced as examples at our request, in drawing and architecture and

Page 145:
Detail of **Virgin and Child with St Anne**, *c. 1502–1513 (?)* *(ill. p. 149)*

Studies and Notes on the Water Balance of the Earth, 1506–1508
Pen and ink, 290 x 220 mm
Seattle, Melinda and William H. Gates III, Codex Leicester, fol. 1B (36r)

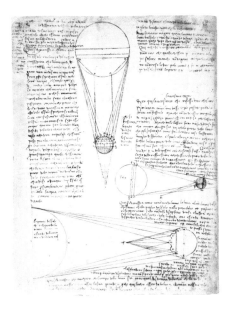

Studies on the Illumination of the Moon, *c. 1506–1508*
Pen and ink, 293 x 221 mm
Seattle, Melinda and William H. Gates III, Codex Leicester, fol. 1A (1r)

Page 147:
Studies on Light and Shade, *c. 1508*
Pen and ink over black chalk, 437 x 314 mm
Windsor Castle, Royal Library (RL 19149v–19152v)

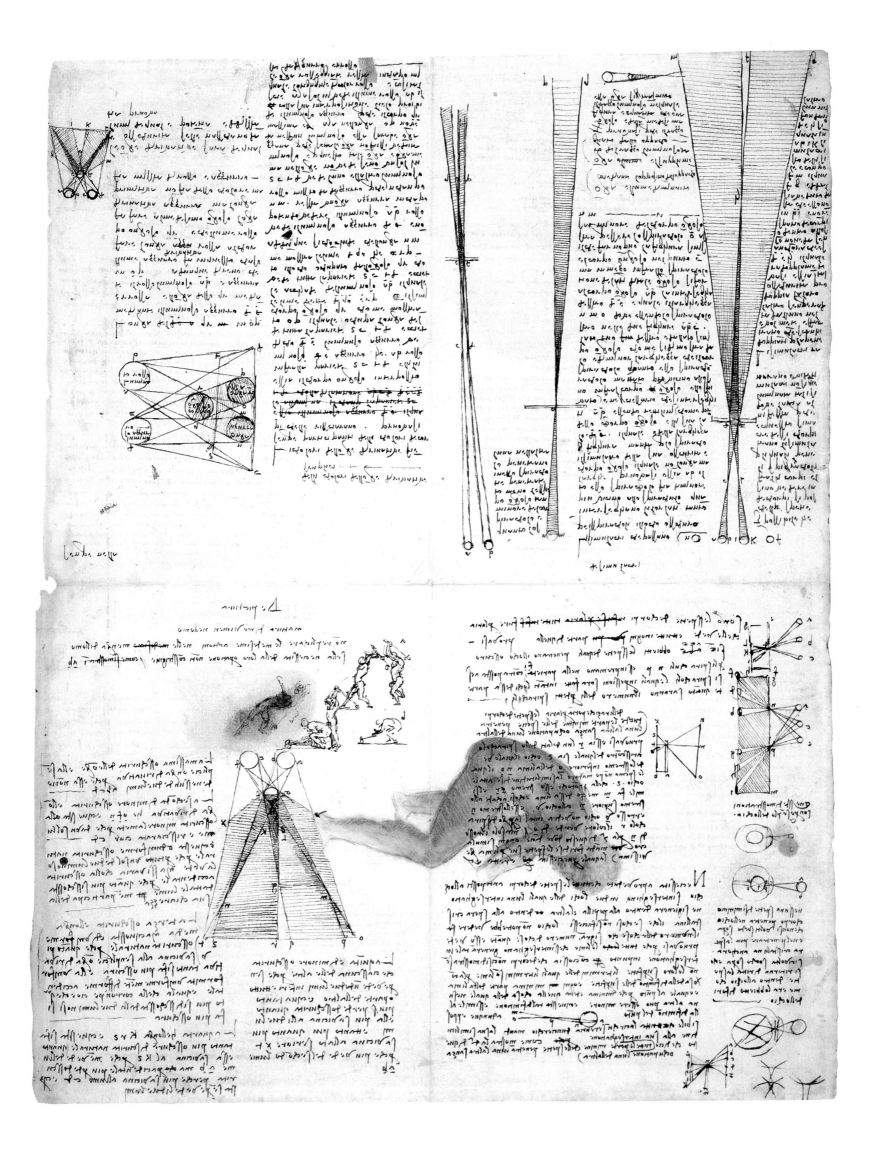

other areas pertinent to our requirements, he satisfied us in a way which not merely matched our expectations but filled us with admiration."

Despite the promises made to Soderini, however, Leonardo's departure from Milan was put off yet again after this letter, following the intervention of the king of France himself. On 12 January 1507 Louis XII informed Francesco Pandolfini, the Florentine envoy at the French court in Blois, that His Majesty wished to meet Leonardo in Milan. Pandolfini reported the king's request, which was evidently issued in the tone of a command, as follows: "This morning, in the presence of the Most Christian King, His Majesty summoned me to him and said: 'Your Signori [government] should write to me. Tell them that I need your painter, master Leonardo, who is living in Milan, because I wish him to make some things for me. See that your Signori charge him with this task and command him to place himself immediately at my service, and that he does not leave Milan before my arrival. He is a good master, and I would like to have a number of things by his hand. And write to Florence in a way that will achieve this end, and do it straight away, and show me the letter being dispatched to Milan.'" Further on, Pandolfini reveals the reason why the king is so eager for Leonardo to enter into his employ in Milan. "All this has been sparked by a small painting by [Leonardo], which arrived here recently and is very greatly admired." The painting in question may have been the – now lost – first version of the *Madonna of the Yarnwinder*, which was probably taken back to France by the man who commissioned it, Florimond Robertet.

Pandolfini goes on to discuss Louis XII's specific intentions. "When I asked His Majesty during our conversation what sort of works he wanted from Leonardo, he replied: 'A number of small pictures of Our Lady and other things, depending on what springs to mind. Perhaps I will also have him paint my portrait.' In a further conversation that I conducted with His Majesty to the benefit of Your Si-gnori, in which I discoursed on Leonardo's perfection and on his other qualities, His Majesty, adding what he had heard about Leonardo, asked me if I knew him. And when I replied that he was a very dear friend of mine, he replied: 'Write a few lines to him straight away and tell him he is not to leave Milan and that Your Signori will be writing to him from Florence.' And for this reason I wrote a note to the aforementioned Leonardo and told him how favourably His Majesty was disposed towards him [...]"

The Florentines were naturally powerless to deny the wishes of Louis XII. Not long after leaving Florence, Leonardo thus found himself in the service of the Milan representative of the French king, from whom, over the following years, he would receive his most regular income yet (RLW § 1529). Our knowledge about Leonardo's second Milanese period, which was interspersed with brief spells in Florence, remains full of gaps, however. What works of art Leonardo produced, and on what other tasks he was engaged, are questions still not fully answered. We know that he continued in Milan, and later in Rome, the anatomical studies that he had resumed in Florence. He also turned his attention to the illumination of the moon (ill. p. 146) and more generally to the effect of light and shadow on three-dimensional bodies (ill. p. 147). During more or less the same period, he designed decorations for festivities at the French court in Milan, made himself useful as an architect, was involved on the expansion of irrigation systems and worked on unfinished compositions such as the *Virgin and Child with St Anne* (Cat. XXVII/ill. p. 149). He had probably already begun this picture in Florence, since in formal terms it is a variation, in reverse, of the St Anne composition begun for the church of SS Annunziata in Florence (Cat. XXII/cf. Ch. VII). The *Virgin and Child with St Anne* today housed in the Louvre may possibly even be identical with a panel (*tavola*) for Louis XII mentioned by Charles d'Amboise in January 1507, or with a painting mentioned by Leonardo himself just over a year later.

Drapery Study for the Virgin and Child with St Anne,
c. 1501 or *c.* 1510/11 (?)
Black chalk, brush, black wash,
white heightening, on white paper,
230 x 245 mm
Paris, Musée du Louvre, Cabinet
des Dessins, Inv. 2257

Studies for the Infant Christ,
c. 1501–1510 (?)
Red chalk and white heightening
on reddish prepared paper,
285 x 198 mm
Venice, Gallerie dell'Accademia,
Inv. 257

Virgin and Child with St Anne, *c.* 1502–1513 (?)
Oil on poplar, 168.5 x 130 cm
Paris, Musée du Louvre,
Inv. 776 (319)

In spring 1508, in a petition probably addressed to Charles d'Amboise, the artist namely wrote: "I am now sending Salaì to you to explain to Your Lordship that I am almost at the end of my litigation with my brothers, and that I expect to find myself with you this Easter, and to bring with me two pictures of Our Lady, of different sizes, which have in my own time been brought almost to completion for our own most Christian King, or for whomsoever Your Lordship pleases. I should dearly like to know where upon my return to you I might have lodgings, for I should not like to trouble Your Lordship further. And also whether having worked for the most Christian King, my salary is to continue or not" (MK § 619).

Leonardo's letter offers a subtle indication that modes of artistic production were beginning to change. In the period around 1500 there was still no art market in the modern sense; as a rule, artists worked exclusively to commission, producing pictures whose destination was known from the outset. They did not, in other words, build up stocks of paintings that could be sold upon demand. In the case of famous artists whose services were sought after by royal patrons, however, this model was gradually beginning to change. A case in point is Leonardo's *Virgin of the Rocks*, which although originally commissioned to form part of an altarpiece by the Franciscan Confraternity of the Immaculate Conception, was sold to a private individual at the instigation of the artists (cf. Ch. III). The ties that had traditionally bound works of art to specific contexts and functions were thus slowly starting to loosen. Further evidence of this process can be deduced from the letters, cited above, by Isabella d'Este and Francesco Pandolfini, which indirectly acknowledge a greater autonomy on the part of the artist: thus both Isabella and the French king are relatively non-specific when it comes to the sorts of artworks they wanted Leonardo to paint for them. Leonardo's response to this shift emerges in his letter to Charles d'Amboise, where we learn that he has produced, on his own initiative, paintings of the Virgin in different sizes, either for Louis XII himself or some other interested party.

Leonardo's *Virgin and Child with St Anne* may be a similar case of a painting originally conceived for a specific context and as the result of a concrete agreement, but then retained in the master's workshop, either as a basis for further copies (see below) or for sale, should the opportunity present itself, to an art lover. This would explain why Leonardo kept the picture in his possession right up to his death. Certain of the painting's formal properties furthermore suggest that the *Virgin and Child with St Anne* was the culmination of many years of work. In terms of its figural composition, its dynamism and its unusual landscape background, the painting indeed has the character of an artistic legacy, an echo of earlier forms. This is true not only of its pyramidal construction, as deployed in earlier paintings (Cat. III, VI, XI, XXII), and its atmospheric background (Cat. III, IV, V, XXIII), but also the arrangement of its figures, which can also be found in previous drawings.

In the *Virgin and Child with St Anne*, Leonardo again employs a sequence of interconnected figures – almost as if St Anne and Mary have the same body, portrayed in two different positions. The compositional relationship between the figures, and the fact that St Anne and Mary appear to be of a similar age, serve to emphasize the close family ties between the individuals portrayed. The youthful appearance of both women can also be interpreted as a reference to their ideal age, which is directly connected to the doctrine that both were virgin mothers. St Anne is portrayed as the same age as Mary because of her *Mariaformitas*, her "likeness to Mary": the Marian attribute of a youthful face is transferred from the Virgin to St Anne in order to underline her rank and saintliness.

Alongside the constellation of its figures and its wealth of movement, another striking feature of the *Virgin and Child with St Anne* is the mountainous landscape, which, somewhat in the manner of a ver-

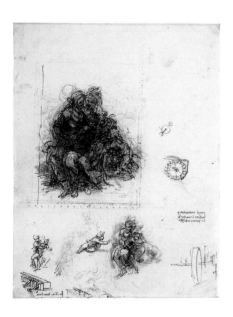

Study for the Virgin and Child with St Anne,
c. 1501 (?)
Pen and ink over black chalk,
260 x 197 mm
London, British Museum,
Inv. 1875-6-12-17r

Study for the Head of Leda,
c. 1505–1510 (?)
Pen and ink over black chalk,
200 x 162 mm
Windsor Castle, Royal Library
(RL 12516r)

tical backdrop, entirely fills the background. The peaks melting into the distant haze form a high horizon; in the right-hand side of the picture they rise even higher than the head of St Anne and appear more monumental than in Leonardo's early paintings. This increased monumentality may be related to the artist's studies into geology and hydrology, or to his views on the endless cycle of nature and the creation of the earth (ill. p. 151). In this context, the chains of mountains in the background might be seen as continents that rose up out of the primeval ocean in prehistory and were eroded over the course of time (RLW § 929, 938, 941, 967, 976). Towards the end of the 1490s Leonardo had observed in this regard that "the summits of mountains for a long time rise constantly" (RLW § 981). A few years later, he described how mountains and strata of rock were created as a result of the erosive action of flowing water: "The water which flowed down from the land exposed by the sea, after the land had risen up out of the sea [...], began to form various streams in the lower parts of this plain [...] These streams then gradually ate away at the banks of the rivers, until the walls of these rivers became steep mountains, and when all the water had flowed away, these mountains began to dry and to form rock in strata of greater or lesser width, depending on the thickness of the mud which the rivers deposited in the sea when they flooded" (Ms. F, 11v). The fissured layers of rock visible at the feet of St Anne and the Virgin correspond with this stratification theory, while the mountains in the background recall the land that in ancient times rose out of the sea, as described by Leonardo in his notes on the power of erosion cited above.

Alongside the geological associations of the background landscape bathed in a luminous haze, we should also note the ways in which, even more than in the *Madonna of the Yarnwinder* (cf. ill. p. 121), the treatment of the background in the *Virgin and Child with St Anne* reflects other of Leonardo's observations of nature and experiments. In no other painting by Leonardo is the luminosity of the sky and the way

in which it appears blue in the distance captured to such atmospheric effect. The blue colour of the air, in particular, was something that Leonardo tried to explain both in his theoretical writings and with the aid of scientific experiments. Thus he observes: "Beyond the sun and us there is darkness and so the air appears blue" (RLW § 868). In another place, he explains that "the atmosphere assumes this azure hue by reason of the particles of moisture which catch the rays of the sun" (RLW § 300). By way of another example of the blue of the atmosphere (RLW § 304), he offers the following observation: "Again as an illustration of the colour of the atmosphere I will mention the smoke of old and dry wood, which, as it comes out of a chimney, appears to turn very blue, when seen between the eye and the dark distance" (RLW § 300). Leonardo believes he has made a similar observation when looking at "the dark shadows of distant mountains when the air between the eye and those shadows will look very blue". In this same passage the artist also explains why the air appears white directly above the horizon and blue further up, namely because directly above the horizon there is more air between the eye and the darker "sphere of fire" higher up.

In considering the *Virgin and Child with St Anne* in terms of Leonardo's observations on the colour of the atmosphere, however, we should not forget that we are here looking at a religious painting, one whose Christian symbolism had already caught the attention of Pietro da Novellara in the example of the first Florentine version of the St Anne cartoon (Cat. XXII/cf. Ch. VII). Thus the Virgin is trying to separate Jesus from the lamb, the sacrificial animal that symbolizes his Passion, while St Anne, as the personification of the Church, is trying in turn to prevent her from doing so, since the Saviour must be allowed to fulfil his destiny on the Cross. As in Novellara's interpretation of the constellation of the figures, so too there is religious symbolism in the background landscape (cf. Ch. III): the emptiness of nature, largely untouched by human hand, the low-lying valley that, although unsuit-

Explosion of Rock caused by the Bursting of a Water Vein, *c.* **1508–1511**
Black chalk, 178 x 278 mm
Windsor Castle, Royal Library
(RL 12387)

[...] it took me about two weeks to paint the splash. I loved the idea, first of all, of painting like Leonardo, all his studies of water, swirling things.

DAVID HOCKNEY, 1976

As for his use of light, it seemed that Leonardo was always anxious not to portray it in all its brightness, as if wishing to reserve it for somewhere more appropriate. He also painted areas of shadow with a great intensity so as to maintain contrasts. Through these skilful means, he arrived at all that nature can achieve in his marvellous representation of faces and bodies. And in this respect he was superior to all, so that in one word we can say that Leonardo's light was divine.

GIAN PAOLO LOMAZZO, 1590

X The last years

nique, an artistic procedure described in antiquity by Pliny and at the end of the Middle Ages by Cennino Cennini and perfected by Leonardo in oil painting. This procedure involves the application of multiple layers of thin, translucent glazes, which give rise within the painting to an extremely wide and subtle range of tonal values. Outlines thereby become blurred into soft transitions from areas of light and dark and hence lend plasticity to the figure being portrayed. The painterly effect of this process depends, amongst other things, on experimentation with oils, which can be carefully built up layer upon layer and which make it possible to arrive at an almost monochrome portrayal of the subject that relies on fine nuances of light and shade alone. In his *St John the Baptist*, Leonardo also deploys *sfumato* as a means of conveying a sophisticated pictorial message: illuminated by a light source that must lie outside the pictorial space, the Baptist emerges from the almost black background as a figure of light. Leonardo thus translates into paint the idea underlying the composition as a whole, namely that John the Baptist is not the source but only the recipient of and witness to God's light, which is shining down on him. The painting thereby lends visual expression to the opening verses of St John's Gospel, which speak of the one who was sent to bear witness to the light. *Sfumato* is thus not simply an autonomous artistic means of expression, but also serves to convey the religious content of the picture. Shadow, the second dominant formal element of the painting, might be understood analogously: it was seen as a symbol of God made flesh in the body of Jesus Christ and thus points, like the light, to the Son of God who will come directly after John. Just like the painting's light, its shade thus also conveys a religious symbolism.

Uncertainty still surrounds the origins of the *St John the Baptist*, since no reliable documentation relating to the date of the painting has survived. The gesture of the right hand would at first sight seem to date the panel to Leonardo's second period in Florence, where the gesture was widely known in art. Thus it is found in St John compositions

from the early 15th century (cf. Ch. II), in Leonardo's own *Adoration of the Magi* and, towards the end of the 1400s, in Domenico Ghirlandaio's panels for the high altar of Santa Maria Novella. But the painting's *sfumato* technique, here taken to its furthermost extreme, and its massive influence on Raphael's Roman works, argue in favour of a later dating. Furthermore, the subject matter itself – John the Baptist as the witness to God's light – is strongly connected with papal Rome, where, as Leo X, Giovanni de' Medici was currently pontiff.

Indeed, the theme of St John the Baptist as the witness to God's light was taken up by Raphael and his workshop in several paintings executed between 1517 and 1518 at the papal court in Rome. One such is the *Young St John* attributed to Giulio Romano (*c.* 1499–1546) and Raphael, which was probably commissioned to mark Pompeo Colonna's election as cardinal (ill. p. 161). Although this large-format canvas differs from Leonardo's *St John* in its composition, the two works nevertheless reveal a number of significant parallels. Thus each portray the saint as a solitary figure, and both are dominated by the contrast between the brightly lit flesh of the saint and the darkness of the background. Giulio Romano was clearly familiar with Leonardo's *St John*, and it would have seemed appropriate to honour the pope indirectly, whose civilian name was Giovanni (John), with a painting of St John as the witness to God's light.

Serving as a witness to the light is also the theme of Raphael's *Portrait of Leo X with Cardinals Giulio de' Medici and Luigi de' Rossi*, executed between 1517 and 1518 (ill. p. 161). Several elements of the composition point to this theme: the pronounced contrast between areas of light and dark, the Bible, which lies open in front of the Pope, and the golden ball topping the back of the papal chair. In the lavishly illuminated Bible, Raphael gives us the opening verses of the Gospel according to St John – "In the beginning was the Word, and the Word was with God" ("In principio erat Verbum et Verbum erat apud Deum") – and thus the beginning of the section that ends with the reminder that John

Old Man Seated on a Rocky Outcrop, seen in right-hand Profile, with Water Studies, *c.* 1513
Pen and ink, 152 x 213 mm
Windsor Castle, Royal Library
(RL 12579r)

Giacomo Salaì (?)
Copy after Leonardo's Annunciation Angel (?), after 1513
Tempera (?) on wood, 71 x 52 cm
Basle, Kunstmuseum

Page 165:
Workshop of Leonardo (?)
St John the Baptist (with the Attributes of Bacchus), *c.* 1513–1519
Oil on wood, transferred to canvas, 177 x 115 cm
Paris, Musée du Louvre, Inv. 780

Today I read Leonardo da Vinci's book on painting and now understand why I have never been able to understand anything in it before.

The complete paintings

The following catalogue raisonné contains the cartoons and paintings by Leonardo da Vinci's own hand, a number of early copies of his lost paintings and cartoons, together with more contentious attributions, insofar as these are rationally justified. Also included are two paintings by Andrea del Verrocchio to which Leonardo is known or at least assumed to have contributed.

I have confined myself as a rule to a brief discussion of the technique, condition, provenance, attribution and patronage of the works in question. More detailed descriptions and interpretations are found, in the majority of cases, in the main text. The sources mentioned in the catalogue section (letters, contracts, poems and early descriptions of paintings) are also cited, in translation, in the main text. The bibliographical references do not aim to be exhaustive. Details relating to the technique in most cases comprise generic descriptions, and not scientific analyses.

In the case of early commentators on Leonardo's works, and specifically Luca Pacioli (1498), Antonio de Beatis (1517), Antonio Billi (active *c.* 1516–1530), Paolo Giovio (*c.* 1523–1527), Sabba da Castiglione (1546) and the Anonimo Gaddiano (*c.* 1537–1547), the reader is referred not to the original sources but to their reproduction in Luca Beltrami (1919), Carlo Vecce (1998, pp. 349–363) and Edoardo Villata (1999).

I Andrea del Verrocchio and Leonardo (?)
Tobias and the Angel, *c.* **1470–1472 (?)**
Tempera on poplar, 84.4 x 66.2 cm
London, National Gallery, Inv. 781

This well-preserved panel incorporates narrow vertical strips of wood pieced onto its left and right-hand sides (1 and 2 cm wide respectively). It was restored in 1867 and 1966. The painting, which may originally have served as a domestic altarpiece, was in the collection of Conte Angiolo Galli Tassi in Florence in the 19th century and was acquired for the National Gallery in London in 1867. Earlier attributions to Antonio Pollaiuolo, Francesco Botticini and Pietro Perugino have now been dismissed.

Its authorship by Verrocchio has been widely accepted, in particular since the detailed analysis by Günther Passavant (1959). Suida (1954), Brown (1998) and Marani (1999) have furthermore sought to prove, on stylistic grounds, that Leonardo was also involved on the painting. These authors consider the dog at Archangel Raphael's feet and the fish held by Tobias to be the work of Leonardo, who is known to have produced studies of animals of a similar kind (the drawings that Marani uses to support his argument date from a later period, however). The attribution of the dog and fish to Leonardo is chiefly based on the claim that Verrocchio was insufficiently experienced in the naturalistic representation of flora and fauna and so turned to his pupil for help. It is an argument that lacks cogency, however, since Verrocchio in fact demonstrates an impressive naturalism in his paintings, as evidenced by his Madonnas in London and Berlin (ill. p. 12).

The picture, which is based on an episode from the Book of Tobit (4: 3–4), owes its origins to the increasing veneration of archangels in Florence in the final third of ßthe 15th century. Antonio del Pollaiuolo's Tobias picture in the Galleria Sabauda in Turin, which originally adorned an interior pillar of Or San Michele in Florence, is considered the formal starting-point for Verrocchio's painting (Passavant, 1959).

Literature: Davies, 1951, no. 781; Suida, 1954, pp. 317–318; Passavant, 1959, pp. 106–121, and 1969, pp. 53–54; no. 19; Brown, 1998, pp. 47–73; Marani, 1999, pp. 28–31, 338.

II Workshop of Andrea del Verrocchio (?)
**Madonna of the Pomegranate
(Dreyfus Madonna),** *c.* **1470–1472 (?) or later**
Tempera and oil (?) on oak, 15.7 x 12.8 cm
Washington, DC, National Gallery of Art, Samuel H. Kress Collection, Inv. 1144 (K1850)

The painting, executed on a single piece of oak, is in good overall condition, although it is somewhat marred by abrasion in the landscape and the Virgin's cloak and neck – something that Shapley (1968) traces back to a restoration of 1930. The problematic nature of this restoration, which sought to "Leonardize" the painting by intensifying its shading, is discussed by Brown (1998).

The painting was auctioned as a work by Leonardo at Christie's in London in April 1864. It passed into the collection of Louis Charles Timbal in Paris, where it was purchased by Gustave Dreyfus in 1872. In 1930 it was sold by his heirs to Joseph Duveen in New York and in 1951 was acquired by Samuel H. Kress, who presented it to the National Gallery. Guiffrey (1908) pronounced the painting to be a work by Lorenzo di Credi, albeit revealing the influence of Andrea del Verrocchio and Leonardo. On the basis of the treatment of the draperies and the composition, Suida (1929) attributed the painting to Leonardo. This attribution was for a long time largely dismissed, but has recently attracted support from Marani (1989 and 1999) and Arasse (1998). Marani sees Leonardesque elements in the painterly treatment of the Virgin's hair and dress and in the technique and ground. The flawed handling of the Child's anatomy, however, and the not particularly Leonardesque character of the background landscape point away from an attribution to Leonardo. Problematic, too, is the wood of which the panel is made: the use of oak as a support was typical neither of Leonardo nor of other painters trained in Florence. Arguing against an attribution to Leonardo is also the fact that the *Dreyfus Madonna* reveals no signs of the fingerpainting found in other early works by Leonardo (cf. Brown, 1998, p. 157; Brachert, 1969, 1974, 1977 and below, Cat. IV–V, VII, IX–X, XIII, XVI).

If its dubious attribution to Leonardo, which Brown (1998) has also recently rejected, were in fact correct, this tiny painting would be of outstanding importance for our understanding of Leonardo's early œuvre. In order to substantiate its still thoroughly uncertain authorship by Leonardo, further evidence of its earlier provenance would also be useful. The possibility cannot be excluded, on the other hand, that the *Dreyfus Madonna* is simply a variation upon a similar Madonna type from Verrocchio's workshop. A comparison might be drawn in this context with the large-format *Madonna* from the circle of Lorenzo di Credi, dating from around 1471, from the monastery of Camaldoli (today in the Museo di Camaldoli), whose provenance can be traced without interruption right back to the 18th century (Smyth, 1979, p. 224; *Maestri e botteghe,* 1992, p. 71). A drawing attributed to Lorenzo di Credi in the Kupferstichkabinett in the Dresden Staatliche Kunstsammlungen (reproduced in Marani, 1999, p. 22) repeats the motif of the *Dreyfus Madonna* almost exactly. This drawing is moreover closely related to the *Madonna of the Carnation* in Munich (Cat. III).

The *Dreyfus Madonna,* in which the Christ Child stands on a parapet in front of the Virgin, corresponds to a type that Leonardo's teacher, Andrea del Verrocchio, developed from formally similar paintings from the workshop of Giovanni Bellini, and which he propagated in Florence at the beginning of the 1470s (Grossman, 1968). Its most interesting facet is the iconographical detail of the open pomegranate, a symbol of the Passion of Christ, which the Virgin holds in her left hand and of which the infant Jesus has taken a seed with his right hand.

Literature: Guiffrey, 1908, pp. 7, 10; Suida, 1929, pp. 15–17; Grossman, 1968; Shapley, 1968, pp. 113–114; Smyth, 1979, pp. 224–229; Marani, 1989, no. 1; *Maestri e botteghe,* 1992, p. 71; Arasse, 1998, pp. 334–336; Brown, 1998, pp. 157–160; Marani, 1999, pp. 18–22.

III Madonna of the Carnation (Madonna with a Vase of Flowers), c. 1472–1478 (?)

Tempera (?) and oil on poplar (?), 62.3 x 48.5 cm
Munich, Bayerische Staatsgemäldesammlungen,
Alte Pinakothek, Inv. 7779 (1493)

The panel, which is made up of two boards, was trimmed on the left by approximately 1.5 cm and on its other sides by a few millimetres. Narrow vertical strips were then later added to the left and right, measuring roughly 1.5 and 0.5 cm respectively. A crack in the bottom right-hand corner, visible only on the back, was repaired in 1913 with two small pieces of wood. At some point in time, part of the back was planed off in an attempt to reduce the panel's pronounced warp. There is noticeable wrinkling of the paint on the front of the panel, caused by early shrinkage of the oil medium and particularly apparent in the face of the Virgin. This wrinkling reflects Leonardo's still experimental handling of oils: in his attempt to prevent his colours from drying too fast and thus to give himself more time to work on the Virgin's face and neck, he probably mixed his pigments with a little too much oil (Sonnenburg, 1983). Leonardo in fact experimented with the use of various oils as binders in the 1470s (Calvi, 1925/1982, pp. 51–52).

For the architectural elements of the middle ground (arcades, window jambs, columns, window seat) Leonardo scored precise underdrawings into the ground, as are also found in the *Adoration of the Magi*, for example (Cat. V). These clean lines, executed with the aid of dividers and a ruler, deviate in places from the outlines in the final painting. A number of pentimenti can be identified in the head and shoulder of the Christ Child (which were both originally larger) and in the Virgin's left shoulder (Möller, 1937, p. 22). The painting was cleaned in 1889/90 by the restorer Alois Hauser, who retouched a few small sections of the background top left and a somewhat larger area lower left, in particular the parts of the ring finger and little finger of the Virgin's right hand where they border onto the left-hand edge of the panel, and part of Jesus's right foot. The Virgin originally held a cloth between the thumb and index finger of her right hand (today barely visible, but reliably documented in a copy of the painting in the Louvre; see below). The Virgin's lower left arm has also been retouched, the red of the fabric evidently having faded (in a similar fashion to the reds in the *Baptism of Christ*, Cat. IV). The gold filigree decoration on the Virgin's sleeve and neckline has also been repainted (information supplied by Jan Schmidt).

The provenance of the *Madonna of the Carnation* cannot be traced very far back. It is first documented in the upper corridor of Wetzler's apothecary shop in Günzburg on the Danube. Yet to be substantiated are suggestions that, prior to this, the painting was located in Burgau Monastery just a few kilometres away, or alternatively that it was brought from Italy by Auxilianus Urbani, an Italian collector who married into the Günzburg apothecary family in 1792 (Möller, 1937). Whatever the case, the painting formed part of the estate of the widow Therese Wetzler and was auctioned after her death for just 22 marks. It was pur-

chased by Albert Haug, who shortly afterwards, in 1889, sold it for 800 marks to the Alte Pinakothek – its valuation price at that time was 8000 marks.

Whether the painting represents the Madonna mentioned by Vasari (1550) as being in the possession of the Medici Pope Clement VII, cannot be stated with certainty. Emil Möller (1937) and David Brown (1998) have nevertheless identified two details which suggest that the picture may have been commissioned by the Medici. Thus the capitals of the two window columns and the pilasters largely correspond to the capitals of Michelozzo's Palazzo Medici in Florence; furthermore, the four glass balls hanging down from a cushion at the very bottom of the panel may be interpreted as *palle medicee* (Medici heraldic devices).

The attribution of the *Madonna of the Carnation* to Leonardo, originally proposed by Adolf Bayersdorfer immediately after purchasing the picture, was at first by no means unanimously accepted. The thorough study of the painting conducted by Möller (1937) eventually allowed the panel to be confidently assigned to Leonardo, an attribution that remained largely unchallenged during the last 30 years of the 20th century and was substantiated afresh by the meticulous study conducted by Brown (1998). Supporting this attribution are, in particular, the insecurity evident in the artist's handling of oils, for which there are no direct parallels in the works of Verrocchio, the masterly treatment of the Virgin's robes and the crystal vase and the atmospheric landscape background. The dating of the painting remains a subject of contention, but in recent literature is placed between 1470 and 1478.

Since Suida (1929, p. 20 and fig. 4), a drawing of the head of the Virgin in the Louvre (Inv. 18 965) has been related by some to the Munich panel. Its attribution to Leonardo is not generally accepted, however. Although Möller (1937, pp. 10–14) refers to a number of original drawings by Leonardo, these correspond only approximately to the final painting. A fairly accurate copy of the painting (wood, 60 x 59 cm), probably by a Northern master of the 16th century (perhaps Johann König, c. 1586–c. 1635, active in Augsburg, Venice and Rome), is housed in the Louvre (Inv. 1603, Béguin, 1983, p. 88). Marani (1999, pp. 38, 73) mentions a further copy in a private collection in Florence and a large-format variation from the circle of Ridolfo Ghirlandaio in the Walters Art Gallery in Baltimore.

Literature: Vasari, 1550, p. 549; Vasari, 1965, p. 260; Möller, 1937; Heydenreich, 1953, I, pp. 33–34, II, p. IV; Kultzen, 1975, pp. 58–60; Sonnenburg, 1983, pp. 24–26, 54–90 and 75; Heydenreich, 1985, pp. 33–36; Brown, 1998, pp. 127–136.

IV Andrea del Verrocchio and Leonardo
The Baptism of Christ, *c.* 1470–1472 and *c.* 1475
Oil and tempera on poplar, 180 x 151.3 cm
Florence, Galleria degli Uffizi, Inv. 8358

The support is composed of a total of six boards, three wider and three very narrow, glued together vertically, whereby the narrow board on the left-hand side is additionally secured with four iron nails. As evident from the borders on all four sides, the panel has not been trimmed. The back reveals a number of brush drawings of nude figures in the manner of the Pollaiuolo brothers and other motifs (Natali, 1998, p. 259); these bear no direct compositional relationship to the *Baptism of Christ*, however. Fingerprints typical of Leonardo are found on the body of Christ (Brown, 1998, p. 136). Small areas of damage – for example in the head of the angel on the left and in the lower section of the painting, where the shrinking of the wood had caused the paint to flake off (Sanpaolesi, 1954) – were retouched when the painting was restored in 1998. The colours have greatly faded in a number of places, for example in Christ's loincloth and John's cloak. Passavant (1959 and 1969) refers to a restoration carried out in the late 19th century, in the course of which the lower section of the painting, Christ's loincloth and the angel on the far left may have been altered, to a degree that can no longer be precisely determined. Following its most recent restoration, the painting now seems altogether more homogeneous than before, albeit also somewhat flatter.

The panel was painted in at least two separate phases by two or even three different artists (*Maestri e botteghe*, 1992, p. 38). Verrocchio is thought to have started the painting in *c.* 1470 or a little later and to have executed the overall composition as well as large parts of the picture in tempera. The underdrawing on the gesso ground, still visible in places, is entirely by his hand. At a later date – *c.* 1475/76 (Kemp, 1981, p. 60) or even as late as *c.* 1480 (Passavant, 1969, p. 196) – the panel was then reworked by Leonardo using oil-based paints, at that time still uncommon in Florence. Following detailed technical analysis, Leonardo is now credited with considerable involvement on the composition: as well as executing the angel on the far left entirely in oils, he also reworked in oils the figure of Christ, originally laid down in tempera by Verrocchio, as well as the river bed and large parts of the background landscape, with the exception of the rocks on the right (Sanpaolesi, 1954; Natali, 1998, p. 66). This discovery falls in line with Vasari's assertion that Leonardo painted the angel in the *Baptism of Christ* on which Verrocchio was working. Recent investigations using infra-red reflectography have revealed that the background above the heads of the two angels originally featured a more conventional landscape, one characterized more by trees than by rocks and water (*Lo sguardo degli angeli*, 1998, pp. 70 and 130).

The painting was first housed in the Vallombrose church of San Salvi, directly outside the walls of Florence. From there it passed to the convent of Santa Verdiana, probably in 1564, to the Accademia di Belle Arti in Florence in 1810 and in 1914 to its present home. Albertini (1510) was probably referring to this painting when he stated that "uno Angelo di Leonardo da Vinci" was to be found in San Salvi. Antonio Billi (p. 61) and the Anonimo Gaddiano (p. 89) also name a *Baptism of Christ* in San Salvi amongst the works of Andrea del Verrocchio. Vasari summarizes the information provided by Albertini, Billi and Gaddiano when he identifies the angel on the far left as the work of Leonardo. Richa's reference (1754, I, p. 395) to the preservation in San Salvi of a relic of St John perhaps provides indirect support for the case for San Salvi as the original destination of the Baptism painting. This leads Passavant (1969, pp. 62 and 58) to conclude that the church of San Salvi may have included a chapel dedicated to St John, for which Verrocchio's painting provided the altarpiece.

Although several of the drapery studies attributed to Leonardo have been related to the angel in the *Baptism of Christ* (von Seidlitz, 1909; Arasse, 1998), none of these studies corresponds accurately enough to the robes of the angel in the painting. Unconvincing, too, is the attempt to relate the drawing of the head of a young man in profile, dated to December 1478, to the angel in the *Baptism of Christ* (von Seidlitz, 1909). Leonardo is believed to have executed his sections of the panel at a relatively late date, for example 1478 (Marani, 1999). Passavant, who conducted a very thorough analysis of the painting, even considers it possible that Leonardo reworked the painting in the early 1480s (Passavant, 1969, p. 196).

As regards who commissioned the painting, Antonio Natali (1998) recently suggested the Vallombrose monk Simone di Michele Cione, who was probably Andrea del Verrocchio's brother. Natali also discusses the iconography of the painting (cf. main text, p. 16), which he sees as drawing not only upon the Gospels (Matthew 3:3–17; Mark 1:9–11; John 1:26–36) but also upon the *Catena aurea* of St Thomas Aquinas.

Literature: Albertini, 1510; Benedettucci, 1991, p. 61 (Billi); Frey, 1892, p. 89 (Anonimo Gaddiano); Gelli, 1896, p. 62; Vasari, 1550, pp. 448–449 and 547; Vasari, 1568, IV, p. 22; Vasari, 1965, p. 258; von Seidlitz, 1909, I, pp. 40–46; Sanpaolesi, 1954, pp. 29–32; Passavant, 1959, pp. 58–88; Passavant, 1969, pp. 57–60 and no. 21; Berti, 1979, p. 588; Kemp, 1981, pp. 58–61; Marani, 1989, no. 6; *Maestri e botteghe*, 1992, p. 38 (N. Pons); Brown, 1998, pp. 27–31, 43, 136–145; Arasse, 1998, pp. 46–52; Natali, 1998; *Lo sguardo degli angeli*, 1998.

V Annunciation, c. 1473–1475 (?)

Oil and tempera on poplar, 100 x 221.5 cm
Florence, Galleria degli Uffizi, Inv. 1618

The relatively well-preserved and fully intact wooden panel (borders on all four sides) consists of five boards, 3.5 cm thick, glued together horizontally. Towards the end of the 19th century, the boards were planed off on the back to reduce their thickness. Several areas of flaking paint, in particular in the architecture behind the Virgin and in the lower part of the wall behind the angel, were retouched when the painting was restored in 2000 (*L'Annunciazione*, 2000, pp. 95–120). This restoration has also rendered more legible the wings of the angel (retouched at some point in the past by another hand), the row of trees and landscape behind the angel and the interior on the right-hand edge of the composition. Since the painting reveals no traces of *spolvero* (pounce powder), it is assumed (Sanpaolesi, 1954) that the underdrawing for the figures was carried out in freehand (the validity of this conclusion, drawn from the absence of *spolvero*, has recently been challenged, however; Keith/Roy, 1995; Hiller von Gaertringen, 2001). Perspective lines were scored directly into the ground, particularly in the right half of the picture. X-rays also reveal the scored outlines of a window in a completely different place, namely parallel to the rear wall. It follows that the stretch of wall leading away from the right-hand foreground behind Mary was not part of the original conception. X-rays have also revealed that the head of the Virgin has undergone significant alterations: the first version of the area around her hair was removed and then completely repainted (Brachert, 1974). The panel also exhibits numerous pentimenti (Sanpaolesi, 1954; *L'Annunciazione*, 2000): the angel's head was originally lower, and the Virgin's right hand shorter, its little finger neither raised nor bent. In the first version, too, her dress was adorned with a chain and decorative pendant. Evidence of Leonardo's characteristic finger-

painting is found in several places within the *Annunciation*, for example on the underside of the lectern, in the head of the angel, in the sky and in the landscape background (Brachert, 1974). These technical details thus show the artist executing his painting in a relatively spontaneous and immediate fashion.

Until May 1867 the painting was housed in the sacristy of the church of San Bartolomeo a Monteoliveto (outside Florence), whose monks believed it to be a work by Domenico Ghirlandaio. It is unclear whether this church was the destination for which the painting was originally intended. After passing into the collection of the Uffizi, the picture was provisionally exhibited as a work by Leonardo. The case for this attribution was greatly strengthened by the publication in 1907 of a pen and ink drawing, housed in Oxford, which is undoubtedly by Leonardo and which is considered a study for the right sleeve of the angel of the *Annunciation*. Leonardo's now widely accepted authorship of the panel is nevertheless rejected by Passavant (1969) and Wasserman (1984). Wasserman sees Leonardo as responsible primarily for the overall layout and points to the weak execution of the head of the angel, which does not bear comparison with the angel in the *Baptism of Christ*.

Consensus regarding the dating of the painting has yet to be reached. Marani (1989) at first proposed a date of c. 1470. Ottino della Chiesa (1967) and, a second time, Marani (1999) date the panel to 1472–1475, a period broadly in line with older research, while Arasse (1998) suggests the years 1473–1475 and Pedretti (1973) assumes a date of c. 1478. On the basis of current scholarship, the traditional dating of the *Annunciation* to c. 1473–1475 or a little later seems the most plausible. The arguments for an early dating are founded on the painting's supposedly flawed perspective. These "errors" (seen in the corner-stones of the building on the right, for example, which appear too long) can be traced at least in part to the fact that the artist constructed his perspective composition from a viewpoint that lies some two to three metres

to the right of the painting and assumes that the viewer is looking slightly up at the painting (*L'Annunciazione*, 2000, p. 37–59). It is by no means, therefore, whether clear distortions in the perspective should really be judged the result of technical incompetence or whether they should be understood as a response to the proposed location of the final painting. Another striking feature of this picture is Leonardo's use of an "out-of-focus" perspective in the background, where blurred and hazy outlines evoke the impression of greater distances (Veltman, 1986). In other respects the linear perspective follows the conventions familiar from Verrocchio's workshop (Kemp, 1990).

The original destination and function of the painting remain the subject of conjecture. The suggestion that, like Baldovinetti's *Annunciation* in San Miniato al Monte in Florence, it formed part of an ensemble still seems the most likely. While the Oxford drawing is firmly accepted as a study for Gabriel's sleeve, attempts to link other drawings by Leonardo with the painting are less convincing. Thus a drapery study in the Louvre, which is regularly related to the Virgin's robes (Ottino della Chiesa, 1967, p. 88), reveals just as many differences as similarities to the final *Annunciation*.

Many elements of the picture, such as the plants, the landscape, the port, the sea and the mountains in the background, are possibly charged with a Marian symbolism (Salzer, 1893, p. 530; Cardile, 1981/82, Liebrich, 1997, pp. 87–88, 158–161; *L'Annunciazione*, 2000, pp. 47–55). It is no more possible to establish the meaning of each individual element, however, than to determine the correct botanical identity of all the plants (Morley, 1979, p. 559).

Literature: Poggi, 1919, p. III; Ottino della Chiesa, 1967, no. 2; Pedretti, 1973, pp. 30–31; Brachert, 1974; Cardile, 1981/1982; Wasserman, 1984, pp. 54–56; Veltman, 1986, pp. 338–345, Pl. 17.2; Marani, 1989, no. 2; Kemp, 1990, pp. 44–45; Liebrich, 1997, pp. 87–88, 158–161; Arasse, 1998, pp. 293–296; Brown, 1998, pp. 75–99; Marani, 1999, pp. 48–62; *L'Annunciazione*, 2000.

VI Benois Madonna, *c.* **1478–1480**
Oil on wood, transferred to canvas, 49.5 x 31 cm
St Petersburg, Hermitage

When the painting was transferred from wood to canvas in 1824, a strip measuring 1.5 cm wide was added to the bottom edge of the composition; the painting was thus originally probably only 48 cm high. The picture, which like many panel paintings transferred to canvas is in only mediocre condition, was given an additional canvas backing in 1924. Infrared reflectography has revealed numerous pentimenti. Thus the head of the Child was somewhat bigger in an earlier draft of the painting, the Virgin probably held in her left hand a small bunch of flowers (rather than the grasses now visible), her hair probably framed her left temple and the sleeve of her right arm may have been somewhat fuller.

The provenance of the *Benois Madonna* can only be traced back as far as the beginning of the 19th century. The painting, which was previously in the possession of A. I. Korsakov (1751/53–1821), is first mentioned in 1827 in an inventory of the collection of Alexander Petrovich Sapozhnikov, which also describes the transfer of the paint to canvas (Kustodieva, 1994). The picture subsequently passed into the collection of Léon Benois. After being exhibited in St Petersburg in 1908/09, the painting was purchased by the Hermitage from M. A. Benois for 150 000 roubles (Poggi, 1919; Kustodieva, 1994).

Passavant (1969) believes that the *Benois Madonna* is

inspired by Desiderio da Settignano's (*c.* 1430–1464) *Panciatichi Madonna*; all other authors see the influence as being the other way round.

The *Benois Madonna* has been attributed to Leonardo by art historians, including even the sceptical Gustavo Frizzoni, from the early years of the 20th century onwards (Gronau, 1912; Poggi, 1919). The dating of the painting, however, remains the subject of controversy even today. Heydenreich (1953) dates the start of work on the panel to 1478 and proposes that Leonardo reworked the painting in 1506 in order to offer it to the king of France (Beltrami, 1919, no. 183; Villata, 1999, no. 240). Arasse (1998) dates the work to 1478–1480, Kemp (1981) to 1480, while Pedretti (1973) sees it in an even later context, believing the composition to contain references to the *Virgin and Child with St Anne*. However, numerous sketches of the Virgin by Leonardo bearing similarities to the *Benois Madonna* can be consistently dated to the years between *c.* 1475 and 1480, suggesting on compositional grounds that the painting dates from this period. At the same time the treatment of its draperies reveals a certain relationship with later paintings such as the *Virgin of the Rocks* (Cat. XI) and the *Portrait of Cecilia Gallerani* (Cat. XIII), so that the possibility that the St Petersburg painting arose during the 1490s cannot be entirely excluded. Its compositional parallels with the *Virgin and Child with St Anne* are less compelling than they seem and cannot be considered grounds for a late dating: Leonardo is known to have taken up earlier motifs on occasions. The plant in the hand of the infant Jesus is probably a crucifer and thus a symbol of the Passion (Suida, 1929, p. 22; Morley, 1979, p. 559).

The *Benois Madonna* corresponds to a type that is found in many of Leonardo's drawings and that was evidently particularly popular. It exists in numerous copies and variations, as found for example in the Gemäldegalerie in Dresden (Lorenzo di Credi), the Galleria Colonna in Rome, the Galleria Sabauda in Turin and the Museum der bildenden Künste in Leipzig (Gronau, 1912).

Literature: Gronau, 1912; Poggi, 1919, pp. IV–V; Heydenreich, 1953, I, p. 210; Passavant, 1969, p. 220; Pedretti, 1973, pp. 27–28; Kemp, 1981, pp. 54–58; Berti, 1984; Kustodieva, 1994, no. 115.

VIIa Portrait of Ginevra de' Benci, *c.* **1478–1480**
Oil and tempera on poplar, 38.8 x 36.7 cm
Washington, DC, National Gallery of Art,
Ailsa Mellon Bruce Fund, 1967, Inv. 2326

Despite the fact that, at some point prior to 1780 (Möller, 1937/38), the panel was cut down by 12 to 15 cm along the bottom and by approximately 1 cm on the right-hand side, the condition of the portrait can be described as good. During the course of restoration in 1991 (Bull, 1992; Gibson, 1991), small areas of damage were discovered and retouched, in particular on the bridge of Ginevra's nose and in the juniper bush just to the left of her head and in the top right-hand corner. As emerges from a comparison with older photographs, the larger of the two trees on the right, beside Ginevra's shoulder, has altered as a result of this restoration: it now lacks a branch on the left and the lower third of its trunk has become distinctly more slender.

As a consequence of its unusual width, the panel, which is about 1 cm thick and consists of a single board, includes a relatively high proportion of pithy sapwood. With the shrinking of the wood, wrinkling (as seen, for example, to the right of Ginevra) appeared early on in the surface of the paint, which contains a high proportion of oil (Möller, 1937/38, p. 188). Papillary lines from the ball of the hand, the fingers and the thumb are found in various parts of the panel, for example between Ginevra's left shoulder and the water (Brachert, 1969). The painting also reveals several pentimenti: the original iris of Ginevra's left eye clearly shows through to the right of the final version. Less obvious is the fact that Ginevra's left cheek was originally a little broader. This portrait and that of Cecilia Gallerani (Cat. XIII) are the only surviving panel paintings by Leonardo that have been demonstrated beyond a doubt to have em-

VIIb Leonardo (?)
Portrait of Ginevra de' Benci, reverse,
c. **1478–1480**
Tempera (and oil?) on poplar, 38.8 x 36.7 cm
On the banderole the beginning of a hexameter:
"VIRTVTEM FORMA DECORAT" ("She
adorns her virtue with beauty"/"Beauty adorns
virtue")

ployed *spolvero* and a cartoon, in this case, for example, along the lower edge of the right eye, on the bridge of the nose, on the upper lip and along the right-hand outline of the face (Gibson, 1991, p. 162; Bambach, 1999, p. 23).

The *Portrait of Ginevra de' Benci* (1457–*c.* 1520) was commissioned, with a likelihood bordering on certainty, by the Venetian diplomat and humanist Bernardo Bembo (1433–1519) during his second stay in Florence, which lasted from July 1478 to May 1480 (Fletcher, 1989; Kress, 1995). The possibility that it was commissioned during Bembo's first stay in Florence, in 1475/76, is less plausible in view of the chronological evolution of Leonardo's paintings. Bembo's personal device (comprising a laurel branch, a palm branch and a motto) is found in a modified form on the back of the portrait. After its completion, the painting evidently remained in Florence, where it is located by artist biographers (Billi, 1527–1530, the Anonimo Gaddiano, 1542–1547, and Vasari, 1550 and 1568). The painting clearly did not go to Venice, either because Bembo didn't pay for it (Fletcher, 1989) or because it was presented as a gift to Ginevra, with whom Bembo enjoyed a poetically inspired platonic relationship (Walker, 1968). The portrait (at this stage considered a work by Lucas Cranach) is definitely known to have been in the possession of Prince Wenzel of Liechtenstein in Vienna (later in Vaduz) from 1733 onwards, but had probably entered the

family collection in the previous century (Möller, 1937/38, p. 207; Brown, 1998). In 1967 the portrait was acquired for the National Gallery in Washington, DC; it was thereby the last original painting by Leonardo to be sold on the open art market.

The painting was attributed to Leonardo, albeit with strong reservations, by Waagen (1866), although this attribution was by no means unanimously accepted. Thus Poggi (1919) was inclined to attribute the portrait to an as yet unidentified artist from the circle of Verrocchio. Only since Emil Möller (1937/38) completed his thorough investigations into the technique of the painting and the person of Ginevra has the portrait been accepted almost unreservedly as a work of Leonardo. This attribution rests primarily on the fact that early sources are comparatively precise in naming the portrait as a work of Leonardo, and also on the fact that the sitter has been confidently identified as Ginevra de' Benci on the basis of the juniper bush (ital. *ginepro*, a play upon the name Ginevra) flourishing behind her head and by the device of Bernardo Bembo on the reverse of the portrait (Möller, 1937/38; Fletcher, 1989). Without the link established between Leonardo and the portrait in the early sources and the identification of the sitter via the juniper bush and Bembo's emblem, however, Leonardo's authorship would probably still be a matter of debate, for it is hard to relate the portrait in stylistic terms to other early works by the artist. In the wake of Möller's analyses, the contributions by John Walker (1968), Jennifer Fletcher (1989) and David A. Brown (1998) have in particular furthered our understanding of the painting.

A silverpoint drawing by Leonardo, which can be dated to *c.* 1478, and which shows a woman's hands as they might be folded in a portrait, has traditionally been associated with the *Portrait of Ginevra de' Benci* and used to reconstruct the missing lower section of the portrait (most recently by Brown, 1998). This portrait drawing, whose format argues against its connection with the *Ginevra de' Benci* (Arasse, 1998), reveals a certain similarity to the so-called *Dama col mazzolino*, a marble portrait bust by Verrocchio (Florence, Bargello), which in turn brings it into line to some extent with the conventions of contemporary Florentine portraiture. The overall layout of the painting nevertheless reveals the influence of Flemish portraiture, as represented for example by Hans Memling's *Portrait of a Man with a Coin of Nero* (Antwerp) and *Portrait of a Young Man* (Florence, Uffizi; ill. p. 36) and by Petrus Christus's *Portrait of a Young Woman* (Berlin; Hills, 1980; Kress, 1995; cf. main text p. 36). The suggestion that the portrait arose in connection with Ginevra de' Benci's marriage to Luigi di Bernardo Niccolini in 1474 (Marani, 1999), or that it was initially envisaged as an engagement portrait, which was then transformed into a

sort of friendship painting for Bembo with the addition of the device on the back (Brown, 1998, 2001), does not strike me as particularly plausible. Furthermore, the painting does not correspond in its details with the pictorial type of the bridal portrait (Kress, 1995).

The composition of the *Ginevra de' Benci* is taken up in a portrait of a woman ascribed to Lorenzo di Credi (New York, The Metropolitan Museum of Art), in which the sitter is also seated in front of a juniper bush. She holds a gold ring in her left hand, which in this case probably identifies the painting as a marriage portrait. For an interpretation, see the commentary on the reverse of the *Portrait of Ginevra de' Benci* and the main text.

The paint on the reverse is badly damaged at the bottom, which may have been one of the reasons why the panel was trimmed. Noteworthy is the tempera-like character of the medium, which Dülberg (1990, p. 24) has also found on the reverse of other portraits. Differences in the painting technique employed on the front and back of the portrait, and the fact that the plants are in part executed by a right-handed artist (Möller, 1937/38), raise some doubts as to whether Leonardo painted the back of the portrait himself. On stylistic grounds, John Shearman (1992, p. 118) considers the reverse to be originally the work of a Venetian artist. Although this suggestion is not backed up by current scholarship, recent investigations have revealed that the inscription originally painted on the back of the portrait read not "VIRTVTEM FORMA DECORAT", but "VIRTV[S ET] HONOR" (Brown, 1998, p. 121). Since this was Bembo's motto, it is possible to speculate that Bembo had perhaps initially commissioned his own portrait from a Venetian artist, the back of which Leonardo then altered and finished off, before proceeding to execute the portrait of Ginevra de' Benci on the front.

References to Ginevra's virtue are yielded by the inscription and by the symbolism of the plants – juniper, laurel and palm – and the painted porphyry marble. Mundy (1988, pp. 38–39) relates the imitation marble to the start of the 35th book of Pliny's *Historia naturalis*, where portraits are discussed immediately after painted stone.

Literature: Benedettucci, 1991 (Billi), p. 102; Frey, 1892, p. 111 (Anonimo Gaddiano); Vasari, 1550, p. 551; Vasari, 1568, IV, p. 39; Vasari, 1965, p. 266; Poggi, 1919, pp. XXII–XXIII; Möller, 1937/38; Walker, 1968; Brachert, 1969; Shapley, 1979, I, pp. 251–255; Cropper, 1986; Fletcher, 1989; Dülberg, 1990, pp. 23–24, 134–124, no. 166; Gibson, 1991; Zöllner, 1994, pp. 63–65; Kress, 1995, pp. 237–255; Arasse, 1998, pp. 402–404; Brown, 1998, pp. 101–121; Bambach, 1999, pp. 23, 100; Marani, 1999, pp. 38–48; Brown, 2001, no. 16.

VIII Lorenzo di Credi, after a design by Leonardo (?)
Annunciation, c. 1478 or 1485
Tempera on poplar, 16 x 60 cm
Paris, Musée du Louvre, Inv. 1602A (1265)

The fully intact panel (with borders on all four sides), which measures some 2 cm in thickness, has suffered from woodworm and the painting itself is in mediocre condition (dalli Regoli, 1966). The panel originally formed the central section of the predella of an altarpiece commissioned from Andrea del Verrocchio *c.* 1475 for the mortuary chapel of Donato de' Medici, who died in December 1474, in Pistoia cathedral (Passavant, 1959, 1969; dalli Regoli, 1966). The unfinished altarpiece remained in Verrocchio's workshop for a long time and was completed by Lorenzo di Credi largely in the period between 1478 and 1486. The two other sections of the predella are today housed in the Liverpool Art Gallery and the Worcester Art Museum.

When the *Annunciation*, together with other paintings from the Campana Collection in Rome, reached the Musée Napoleon III in 1861 and in 1863 passed from there to the Louvre, it was initially attributed to Domenico Ghirlandaio, then to Lorenzo di Credi

and finally to Leonardo. This last attribution, which possibly goes back to a local tradition in Pistoia (Salvi, 1656–1662), has always met with opposition, for example from dalli Regoli (1966), who points to the technical affinity of the present painting with Credi's predella panel in Worcester. Recently, however, alongside Ottino della Chiesa (1967), Pedretti (1973) and Marchini (1985), a number of advocates of Leonardo's authorship have emerged. In connection with this possible attribution, Marani (1999, pp. 67–69) cites a drawing in the Uffizi ([428E recto] Inv. 328E recto), which is occasionally linked with Leonardo. Quite apart from the fact that its authorship is entirely unsubstantiated, however, its large format rules it out as a preliminary study for the small predella panel (Brown, 1998).

Previous attributions to a single or several artists (Verrocchio, Lorenzo di Credi, Leonardo) pose a number of difficulties. It is hard to imagine, for example, how several artists, amongst them Leonardo, could have worked on such a small predella panel. It is equally hard to position this *Annunciation* within the chronology of Leonardo's early works: supporters of the attribution favour a date between 1478 and 1480, something impossible to marry from a stylistic

point of view with the *Portrait of Ginevra de' Benci* from this same period, which is technically clearly superior to the Paris *Annunciation.* The latter's use of very coarse pigments also speaks against Leonardo's authorship of the painting (Hours, 1954). The only alternative would be to date the *Annunciation* considerably before 1478, which is equally out of the question since even the main altarpiece was at that stage still unfinished. A more sensible solution would seem to be the suggestion, made most recently by Arasse (1998), that the panel was executed by Lorenzo di Credi after a design by Leonardo. This is supported by its compositional similarity to the Uffizi *Annunciation* attributed more plausibly to Leonardo (Cat. V). In view of the above arguments, the picture should be dismissed once and for all from Leonardo's œuvre.

Literature: Salvi, 1656–1662, II, p. 422; Poggi, 1919, pp. II–III; Hours, 1954, pp. 21–22; dalli Regoli, 1966, pp. 111–114, no. 32; Ottino della Chiesa, 1967, no. 11; Passavant, 1969, p. 212; Pedretti, 1973, pp. 29–30; Béguin, 1983, p. 90; Arasse, 1998, p. 46; Brown, 1998, pp. 151–157; Marani, 1999, pp. 67–68.

IX St Jerome, *c. 1480–1482*
Oil and tempera on walnut, 102.8 x 73.5 cm
Rome, Pinacoteca Vaticana, Inv. 40337

The panel, made up of two boards of different widths and planed off on the back, has suffered badly from woodworm. The paint extends all the way to the edges of the panel (information kindly supplied by Arnold Nesselrath, Rome). At some unknown point in time, the head of St Jerome and two neighbouring sections of the panel were sawn out of the painting. The individual parts were later pieced back together again. The panel reveals damage in a number of places, particularly in the lion's back and the rocks on the left-hand edge of the painting (Colalucci, 1993). It was last restored in 1930 and 1993.

Like the *Adoration of the Magi* (Cat. X) probably executed just a little later, the *St Jerome* for the most part gets no further than the design stage. Only the head of the saint, his right leg and parts of the landscape are developed in underpainting. There are no signs of the use of an auxiliary *spolvero* cartoon (Bambach, 1999, p. 23). The design of a crucifix on the right-hand edge of the picture was scored directly into the ground. Leonardo has rubbed the paint with his hand in a number of places, for example in the background, and thereby anticipates the impression of flowing transitions (*sfumato*) for which he would later become famous. *St Jerome* thus provides another example of the fingerpainting and handpainting tech-

nique already seen in the *Portrait of Ginevra de' Benci* (Cat. VII; Brachert, 1969; Colalucci, 1993). Beneath the layer of paint in the left-hand background, above the horizon, is the sketch of a palm tree.

The provenance of the *St Jerome* cannot be traced with certainty beyond the first quarter of the 19th century. The painting is first mentioned in the second volume of Carl Friedrich von Rumohr's *Italienische Forschungen*, published in 1827 (II, p. 308). Rumohr had seen it in Rome in the possession of Cardinal Joseph Fesch, in whose estate it was still to be found upon his death in 1839. Between 1846 and 1857 the cardinal's heirs sold the *St Jerome* to Pope Pius IX. Since then the painting has remained in the uninterrupted possession of the Pinacoteca Vaticana. The *St Jerome*, together with the *Benois Madonna* and the *Portrait of Cecilia Gallerani*, numbers amongst the few paintings by Leonardo that have been loaned out to exhibitions in recent years (for example to Tokyo in 1993 and to Bonn in 1998).

The persuasive arguments expounded by Ost (1975, pp. 8–9) have cast doubt on the view, still held by some (Marani, 1989; Arasse, 1998, p. 344), that the *St Jerome* formed part of the collection of Angelica Kauffmann in Rome at the start of the 19th century. More fiction than fact is similarly the story put about by Cardinal Fesch (Poggi, 1919), who claimed to have discovered the main section of the sawn-up painting in Rome *c.* 1820 and then to have purchased the head of the saint a few years later from a Roman cobbler, who was using it as the seat of a stool. The claim by Ottino della Chiesa (1967) that Leonardo's *St Jerome* formed the basis of an engraving of 1784 by C.G. Gerli is also untenable. Gerli's illustration of a St Jerome is in fact based on drawings from Leonardo's circle (Ost, 1975, p. 7; Marani, 1989).

The early sources contain no references to Leonardo's *St Jerome*. In an inventory compiled by Leonardo in Milan in or after 1495, the artist mentions "certain figures of Saint Jerome" (RLW § 680), but whether the panel today housed in the Vatican was amongst them is doubtful to say the least. The *St Jerome* nevertheless seems to have been known in Milan towards the end of the 15th century (Marani, 1989). It is also unclear whether the Vatican painting is identical with one of the two St Jerome pictures mentioned as forming part of Salaì's estate in 1525 (Shell/Sironi, 1991, pp. 104–105; Villata, 1999, no. 333). Leonardo's painting thus appears to have left virtually no traces in the history of art. Despite its mysterious past and fictitiously embellished provenance, the *St Jerome* – together with the *Adoration, Last Supper* and *Mona Lisa* – numbers amongst the paintings whose attribution to Leonardo has never been seriously doubted.

There is widespread agreement, too, regarding the dating of the painting. On the basis of its similar ground and the identical manner in which the composition is sketched, it is assumed to have arisen in the same period as Leonardo's *Adoration*, which was commissioned in March 1481 and was left unfinished in Florence in 1482. The *St Jerome* was probably commenced before the *Adoration*, for the large-format painting for the monks of San Donato would hardly have allowed him time for a further commission. Indeed, the contract for the *Adoration* expressly stipulates that Leonardo is not to take on any other commissions (Beltrami, 1919, no. 16; Villata, 1999, no. 14). Since the rock formations in the *St Jerome* resemble those of the *Virgin of the Rocks* (Cat. XI), however, the possibility that the picture arose at the start of Leonardo's first Milan period cannot be entirely excluded.

The composition of the *St Jerome* is derived from a kneeling figure (modelled out of wax, wood or clay) commonly found in Quattrocento workshops (Ost, 1975). Ost further claims that Vitruvius's theory of proportion, to which Leonardo devoted himself in 1490, is already reflected in the measurements of the *St Jerome*, but his thesis is undermined by the inaccuracy of these measurements. Leonardo's picture is based in formal terms upon older interpretations of the subject and upon the writings of Jerome himself, in which the saint describes his penance in the desolate wilderness and at the foot of a cross, here barely visible on the right-hand edge of the painting (Rice, 1985, pp. 78–79; cf. main text, p. 47). The inclusion of the lion as the saint's attribute also falls in line with pictorial convention.

The *St Jerome* may possibly have been intended for the Ferranti chapel in the Badia in Florence (Cecchi, 1988), which Filippino Lippi subsequently furnished with an altarpiece of the same subject *c.* 1489/90 (Scharf, 1935, pp. 26–27). This suggestion is lent credence by the fact that Filippino Lippi also took over similar commissions for the chapel of St Bernard in the Palazzo Vecchio in Florence and for San Donato a Scopeto, both of which were originally awarded to Leonardo but which the latter failed to complete. If the *St Jerome* was indeed destined for a side altar in the Badia, the commission was probably secured by Leonardo's father, Piero da Vinci, whose family had maintained a tomb in the Badia since 1472 (von Seidlitz, 1909, I, pp. 10 and 379; Zöllner, 1995, pp. 60–61).

Literature: Poggi, 1919, pp. V–VI; Ottino della Chiesa, 1967, no. 13; Ost, 1975; Rice, 1985; Cecchi, 1988, p. 70; Marani, 1989, no. 8; Colalucci, 1993; Zöllner, 1995, pp. 60–61; Arasse, 1998, pp. 344–350; *Hochrenaissance im Vatikan*, 1998, pp. 552–553.

XIII Portrait of Cecilia Gallerani (Lady with an Ermine), 1489/90

Oil on walnut, 55 x 40.5 cm
Cracow, Muzeum Narodowe, Czartoryski Collection,
Inv. 134

The panel, which consists of a single piece of wood, in all probability comes from the same tree as the support of the so-called *Belle Ferronière* in the Louvre (Cat. XV). Apart from a few small areas of damage, the painting, which retains its original dimensions (borders on all four sides), is in very good condition. The paint, which is built up somewhat higher in the areas of flesh than elsewhere, is evenly applied in a manner similar to the equally well preserved *Mona Lisa* (Cat. XXV). Remains of *spolvero* are found in the outlines of the figure and head and in the drawing within the face, while traces of underdrawing scored directly into the ground can be identified above all in the right arm, right hand, left hand, bridge of the nose and start of the hair (Fabjan/Marani, 1998, pp. 76–77, 83–90; Bambach, 1999, p. 23). The fingerprints typical of Leonardo's painting from this period can be identified in Cecilia's face and on the ermine's head (Brachert, 1977, p. 99).

The background was originally probably of a harmonious shade of grey-blue, later completely repainted in a dark colour (Fabjan/Marani, 1998, p. 87). The theory, often repeated, that the right-hand background once showed an open window (Marani,

1989) was not confirmed by recent research (Fabjan/ Marani, 1998, pp. 82–84). An inscription top left ("LA BELLE FERONIERE / LEONARD D'AWIN-CI") was probably added in the early 19th century.

The painting is described in a sonnet (cf. main text p. 86), published in 1493, composed by the court poet Bernardo Bellincioni, who died in 1492, and is mentioned in 1498 in correspondence between Isabella d'Este and Cecilia (Beltrami, 1919, nos. 88–89; Villata, 1999, nos. 129–130), in whose possession the portrait seems to have remained until her death in 1536. The picture possibly surfaces in the collection of Rudolf II in Prague in 1612. Towards the end of the 18th century, it was purchased in Italy by Prince Adam Jerzy Czartoryski as a present for his mother (Shell/Sironi, 1992). The portrait is documented in the collection of the Czartoryski princes in Puławy from 1809 onwards (Poggi, 1919, pp. XVIII–XIX). Between 1830 and 1876 it accompanied its owner to Paris and then Cracow, where it went on public display in 1882. In autumn 1914, following the outbreak of the First World War, it passed to the Gemäldegalerie in Dresden, but in 1920 returned to Cracow. In 1939 it was taken as war booty to Berlin, where it was exhibited in the Kaiser-Friedrich-Museum. It was also earmarked for the "Führer's Museum" planned in Linz. It was returned to the Muzeum Narodowe in 1946 (Fabjan/Marani, 1998, pp. 78–79).

As in the case of the *Portrait of Ginevra de' Benci* (Cat. VII) and the *Madonna of the Carnation* (Cat. III), the attribution of the *Portrait of Cecilia Gallerani* to Leonardo came to be widely accepted only in the 20th century. After Paul Müller-Walde drew attention to the painting in 1889, in 1900, at the 3rd Congress of Polish Art Historians in Cracow, Jan Boloz-Antoniewicz linked it with the portrait of Cecilia Gallerani attributed to Leonardo in the sources. When war broke out, the painting was evacuated to Dresden, where it subsequently went on show. This intensified the debate over its authorship, which was increasingly attributed to Leonardo (Poggi, 1919). This trend continued between the wars and after the Second World War. No one today doubts the attribution to Leonardo, which as in the case of the *Portrait of Ginevra de' Benci* is supported by a wealth of information pertaining to the sitter.

The *Cecilia Gallerani* has appeared in a relatively large number of exhibitions over the past decades: in Warsaw in 1952, in Moscow in 1972, in Washington, DC, in 1991/1992, in Malmö in 1993/1994, in Rome and Milan in 1998 and in Florence in 1999. No other painting by Leonardo travelled the world so widely in the 20th century.

As in the case of the *Ginevra de' Benci* and the *Mona Lisa*, we are well informed about the young woman in the portrait (Shell/Sironi, 1992; Moczulska, 1995; Fabjan/Marani, 1998, pp. 51–65 [J. Shell]). She was born Cecilia Bergamini in 1473 and in 1483, at the age of 10, was formally ("pro verba") betrothed to Giovanni Stefano Visconti. After this betrothal was dissolved in 1487, and at the latest in 1489, Cecilia became the mistress of Ludovico il Moro, whom she bore a son, Cesare, on 3 May 1491. In July 1492 Cecilia married Ludovico Carminati. She died in 1536.

The animal in Cecilia's arms, zoologically not altogether correctly described as an ermine, was considered a symbol of purity and virtue. It also served as a reference to Ludovico Sforza, Cecilia's lover and the man who commissioned the portrait. The ermine, in Greek *galée*, is also seen as a play upon the name Cecilia Galle-rani. The presence of this symbolic animal has led the portrait to be interpreted in numerous ways, of which we may summarize the most important here: Carlo Pedretti (1990) sees in the portrait a political allegory of the relationship between Ferdinand I of Naples and Ludovico il Moro, whom Ferdinand appointed a member of the Order of the Ermine in 1488. A very different train of thought is pursued by Krystyna Moczulska (1995), who examines the significance of the ermine and the weasel in classical literature and in popular belief and who relates the symbolic animal directly to Cecilia's personal situation, namely her pregnancy. Cecilia is thus connected with the story of Alcmena in Ovid's *Metamorphoses* (9.283–323) and Aelian's *De natura animalium* (2.37). Alcmena was made pregnant by Zeus, whose wife Hera tried to prevent the birth of her child, Hercules. Hera was thereby aided by the servant Galanthis, whom she subsequently turned into a weasel. In late 1489/early 1490 Cecilia and Ludovico il Moro found themselves in a similar situation: Cecilia was pregnant by her lover Ludovico, who was shortly due to marry Beatrice d'Este, for whom the imminent birth of an illegitimate child sired by her future husband was a vexation. According to popular belief, finally, the weasel was an animal that protected pregnant women.

Literature: Bellincioni, 1493, c. 6v–7r (Beltrami, 1919, pp. 207–208; Villata, 1999, no. 72c); Beltrami, 1919, nos. 88–89; Poggi, 1919, pp. XVIII–XIX; Suida, 1929, pp. 91–93; Villata, 1999, no. 129; Kwiatkowski, 1955; Marani, 1989, no. 12; Brown, 1990; Pedretti, 1990; Bull, 1992; Shell/Sironi, 1992; Moczulska, 1995; Fabjan/Marani, 1998.

XIV Giovanni Antonio Boltraffio (?),
after a design by Leonardo
Litta Madonna, *c.* 1490
Tempera (and oil?) on wood, transferred
to canvas, 42 x 33 cm
St Petersburg, Hermitage, Inv. 249

Despite having been transferred from panel to canvas in 1865 and having suffered some damage to the Virgin's cloak, the picture is in comparatively sound condition. Owing to relatively pronounced abrasion of the top layer of paint, however, it today gives a somewhat flat impression.

Compared with other small-format Madonnas by Leonardo, the painting can claim a relatively well-documented provenance. In 1784 it was purchased from Giuseppe Ro by Prince Belgioso; in 1813 it passed into the collection of the Litta family in Milan and in 1865 was sold by Antonio Litta to Tsar Alexander II. Earlier references to the painting must be considered unreliable: it is doubtful, for example, whether this is the same panel seen in 1543 in the Contarini collection in Venice by Marcantonio Michiel (Frimmel, 1888, p. 110). The Madonnas possibly explored in a drawing of 1478 and listed by Leonardo in the Codex Atlanticus of *c.* 1482 (324r/ 888r, RLW § 680) cannot be credibly linked to the *Litta Madonna*, since the painting cannot have arisen prior to Leonardo's first Milanese period.

According to the latest scholarship, the attribution of this Madonna to Leonardo can no longer be upheld. The existence of preliminary drawings in Leonardo's own hand nevertheless imply that the artist was involved in its design. Two of these drawings, in Paris and Frankfurt, can be dated to *c.* 1490, which is now assumed to be the date of the painting itself. Two further preparatory drawings for the *Litta*

Madonna – a drapery study in Berlin (Kupferstich-kabinett, Inv. 4090) and a head of the Christ Child in Paris (Fondation Custodia, Inv. 2886) – are attributed to Leonardo's pupil Giovanni Antonio Boltraffio. Detailed studies by Brown (1990) and Fiorio (2000) have concluded that the painting was executed by one of Leonardo's pupils, based on designs by the master and under his direct supervision, as evidenced by the above-mentioned drawings. It is likely that this pupil was Boltraffio. This theory is supported by the figural type employed for the Christ Child, which is similar to that found in other works by Boltraffio.

Important early copies and variations upon the *Litta Madonna* are found in the Fogg Art Museum in Cambridge, Mass., and in the Castello Sforzesco (Fiorio, 2000, D5, D15) and Museo Poldi Pezzoli in Milan. In the late 1400s or early 1500s Zuan de Andrea made the composition the subject of an engraving and thereby created one of the earliest reproductions of a Leonardo work (Bartsch, 1811, vol. XIII, p. 298, no. 225; after Kustodieva, 1994). An overview of these copies and variations can be found in Gukovskij (1959, p. 77).

Literature: Poggi 1919, pp. 40, XXXIV and LXI; Gukovskij, 1959; Béguin, 1983, p. 84; Pedretti, 1989; Sedini, 1989, pp. 198–199; Brown, 1990; *Leonardo & Venezia*, 1992, no. 74 (D. A. Brown); Kustodieva, 1994, no. 116; Fiorio, 2000, no. A3 and pp. 16, 27–29.

XV Portrait of an Unknown Woman
(La Belle Ferronière), *c.* 1490–1495
Oil on walnut, 63 x 45 cm
Paris, Musée du Louvre, Inv. 778

Apart from small areas of damage on the sitter's décolletage and forehead, the painting is in good condition. The walnut panel probably originates from the same tree as the *Portrait of Cecilia Gallerani* (Cat. XIII; Fabjan/Marani, 1998), which suggests a dating of not much later than 1490. The paint is applied in a manner and depth similar to the *Cecilia Gallerani*. A very

fine craquelure is apparent in particular in the areas of the flesh, whereby it differs from the craquelure found in the *Cecilia Gallerani* and *Mona Lisa* in the unevenness of its distribution (Wolters, 1952, p. 144). There are signs of retouching on the left-hand side of the face – where the hair originally did not extend quite so far down (Wolters) – and on the edge of the lower jaw. Hours (1954) also considers the band across the forehead – a *ferronière* (see below) – to be a later addition.

The provenance of the *Belle Ferronière* can probably be traced back to the time of François I, albeit not entirely smoothly. In *c.* 1542 the painting was apparently one of a number of works by Italian masters – including the *Virgin of the Rocks* and *St John the Baptist* – adorning the *appartement des bains* in François I's Fontainebleau palace (Dimier, 1900, p. 281; Brejon de Lavergnée, 1987, p. 100). The first incontestable proof of its whereabouts, however, is supplied only a century later by Père Dan, who saw the portrait in the royal collection at Fontainebleau in 1642. Towards the end of the 17th century the painting was transferred to the collection of Louis XIV in Paris, before travelling in 1692 to Versailles, where it remained until 1784 (Poggi, 1919). In the 19th century the *Belle Ferronière* is listed in every Louvre inventory (Brejon de Lavergnée). It is not impossible, finally, that the "Florentine lady" seen by Antonio de Beatis in Leonardo's Cloux workshop in October 1517 was in fact the *Belle Ferronière* (Villata, 1999, no. 314).

The very high quality of the painting, the similarities in technique that it shares with other paintings by Leonardo and the fact, mentioned above, that its walnut support was probably cut from the same tree as that used for the *Portrait of Cecilia Gallerani*, leave little doubt that this is a work by Leonardo. And indeed, with the exception of Goldscheider (1960, p. 198),

Wasserman (1984) and Béguin (1983), it is accepted whole-heartedly or with just a few reservations by the majority of modern critics. The identity of the sitter remains unclear, however. Carlo Amoretti (1804) suggested Lucrezia Crivelli, who was the mistress of Ludovico il Moro from *c.* 1495. The Codex Atlanticus (167v–c/ 456v) contains some Latin verses that were probably composed around this same period (Amoretti, 1804, p. 31; RLW § 1560 [incomplete]; PRC, II, pp. 386–387). To link these verses with the *Belle Ferronière*, however, means accepting the relatively late date for the portrait of *c.* 1495. It is also possible, however, to see the young woman in the portrait as Beatrice d'Este or as Cecilia Gallerani, now a few years older (Ottino della Chiesa, 1967).

The story, regularly repeated in the literature of recent years, that the *Belle Ferronière* owes its title to having been confused with another painting (Ottino della Chiesa, 1967; Brejon de Lavergnée, 1987, nos. 16 and 17; Marani, 1989), may not fit the facts; the name may equally well derive from the brow band, or *ferronière*, which is worn by the sitter and which was especially popular in Milan (Goldscheider, 1960). In compositional terms, the painting is closely related to a portrait type found across northern Italy, in which a stone parapet separates the viewer from the pictorial space. This same type surfaces in the works of Antonello da Messina and Giorgione, for example, and is ultimately indebted to earlier Flemish models.

Literature: Dan, 1642, p. 132; Amoretti, 1804, p. 31; Poggi, 1919, pp. XXXII–XXXIII; Suida, 1929, pp. 93–95; Hours, 1954, pp. 22–23; Goldscheider, 1960, p. 198; Ottino della Chiesa, 1967, no. 28; Béguin, 1983, p. 81; Brejon de Lavergnée, 1987, no. 16.

XXIII Giacomo Salaì (?), after a design by Leonardo
Madonna of the Yarnwinder,
c. 1501–1507 (?)
Oil on wood, 50.2 x 36.4 cm
New York, Private Collection

XXIV Workshop of Leonardo,
after a design by Leonardo
**Madonna of the Yarnwinder, 1501–1507
or later (?)**
Oil on wood (poplar?), 48.3 x 36.9 cm
*Drumlanrig Castle, Scotland, In the collection
of The Duke of Buccleuch & Queensberry, KT*

Despite having been transferred first from its original wood panel to canvas and then in 1976 back to panel, the painting is in good condition. In the course of restoration in 1976 and its transferral back to panel, a pentimento was discovered, revealing that Christ's left leg was originally positioned further to the left. At the same time, it was also established that three strips of canvas had been glued onto the original wood panel prior to the application of the ground – a procedure highly unusual for Leonardo but widespread in medieval Tuscan painting. In a restoration undertaken before 1911, several areas of overpainting were removed, namely a loin cloth covering Christ's genitals and some retouching to Mary's left hand and beneath the right foot of the Child (Möller, 1926, p. 67). Infra-red reflectography of the New York *Madonna of the Yarnwinder* has revealed an underdrawing that differs in one important detail from the composition visible today: a group of figures was originally planned beside the Virgin's right shoulder (Kemp, 1994, fig. 33–34). This group of figures was either intended to portray a Nativity (Gould, 1992) or the Virgin and Child with Joseph, who is making a playpen or crib for his foster son (Kemp, 1992, pp. 269–270; Bury, 1992, p. 188). A corresponding scene is found in the background of several copies of the painting (Vezzosi, 1983, ill. 53–56).

The provenance of the small-format panel can be traced back to Henry Petty-Fitzmaurice, the third Marquis of Landsdown, who purchased the painting in 1809 – so at least runs the catalogue accompanying the Giffard Sale of 1879 at Christie's in London. The painting, attributed to Leonardo, was sold by Christie's to Cyril Flower, later Lord Battersea, from whom it passed in 1908 to Nathan Wildenstein and René Gimpel in Paris, and in 1928 to Robert Wilson Redford in Montreal. In 1972 it was sold to its present owner. Since then the painting has frequently gone on public display: in Vinci in 1982, in Naples in 1983, in Rome in 1984, in Edinburgh in 1992 (in the company of the Buccleuch version, Cat. XXIV) and in Arezzo in 2000 (Starnazzi, 2000, p. 64).

Following the sale of the *Portrait of Ginevra de' Benci* (Cat. VII) to the National Gallery in Washington, DC, in 1967, the New York *Madonna of the Yarnwinder*, together with the Buccleuch version (Cat. XXIV) of the same subject, currently remains the only privately-owned painting that some established art historians believe may be linked directly with Leonardo (an overview is provided by Vezzosi, 1983, p. 68; Bury, 1992; Gould, 1992). The debate that erupted afresh in particular following the Edinburgh exhibition of 1992 has yet to produce a consensus on the question of attribution. After a comparison with the *Mona Lisa*, commenced only shortly afterwards, and in view of the description of the original in the sources (see below), it must be concluded, however, that the *Madonna of the Yarnwinder* is a workshop product. Only the design stems from Leonardo; the actual painting was carried out largely by an assistant (with the two most likely candidates being Sodoma or Salaì). The underdrawings revealed by infra-red reflectography nevertheless make it clear that the present painting is not a copy executed at a much later date.

Leonardo started work on the composition of the *Madonna of the Yarnwinder* in the spring of 1501 for Florimond Robertet, secretary to the king of France. We owe this information to a letter by Pietro da Novellara of 14 April 1501 (Beltrami, 1919, no. 108; Villata, 1999, no. 151), in which the painting is described and interpreted (cf. main text, p. 127). In his highly detailed description, Novellara also mentions a little basket of yarns (*canestrino dei fusi*) on which the infant Jesus is resting his foot. Since this basket appears neither in the two best versions of the painting nor in infra-red reflectograms, Leonardo's original painting must be considered lost. A final reference to a lost original is possibly found in a letter by Francesco Pandolfini of 12 January 1507 (Beltrami, 1919, no. 183; Villata, 1999, no. 240). The letter refers to a small picture by Leonardo that is housed in Blois and that the French king considers to be exceptionally fine.

Yet to be fully answered is the recently raised question (Starnazzi, 2000) as to whether the mountains in the background draw upon the topography of the Aretine hinterland. The processes of erosion that can be observed in the foothills of the Apennines may well have influenced Leonardo's portrayals of mountains. Not in doubt, however, is the connection between the mountains in the *Madonna of the Yarnwinder* and the landscape background of the *Mona Lisa* and the *Virgin and Child with St Anne*. This connection raises a number of questions with respect to the dating of the painting. While it must have been painted after April 1501, just how much later is difficult to determine. Whatever the case, the underdrawing visible in infra-red reflectograms suggests that the New York version of the *Madonna of the Yarnwinder* arose within Leonardo's immediate circle (Kemp, 1994), and probably not all too long after Robertet's original commission, leading Arasse (1998) to date the present painting to the period between 1501 and 1507. A similar dating is suggested by Pandolfini's letter of 1507, mentioned above. The *Madonna of the Yarnwinder* would thereby call into question the late dating currently accepted for the landscape in the *Mona Lisa*, since the bridge visible in the present background presupposes a familiarity with a similar bridge in the *Mona Lisa* (cf. Cat. XXV).

A red chalk drawing by Leonardo in Windsor Castle is generally accepted as a preliminary study for the *Madonna of the Yarnwinder*; a variation upon this drawing in Venice (Accademia, no. 141) is by a different hand. Further drawings from Leonardo's circle, together with numerous painted versions of varying degrees of quality, are found in Vezzosi (1983, pp. 62–65) and in the catalogue section in Kemp (1992). The authenticity of many of these copies and variations needs to be reviewed, however.

The background of the small-format picture (Cat. XXIV) has in the past been extensively retouched. The area of water behind the Virgin's head, in particular, was added at a later date. Large sections of the middle ground, which also appears to have been re-worked at a later stage, give the impression of being unfinished. Möller (1926, p. 67) believed that the original landscape beneath the overpainting was executed by Leonardo himself. The Virgin and Child appear to have undergone significantly less revision. The Virgin's blue cloak, which has darkened with age, is furrowed almost everywhere with large cracks in the manner of a craquelure caused by early paint shrinkage.

This version of the *Madonna of the Yarnwinder* is first documented in the collection of the Duc d'Hostun et de Tallard, from where, in 1756, it passed into the possession of George Montague. Since 1767 the painting has formed part of the collection of the Dukes of Buccleuch (Kemp, 1992, and 1994, p. 262). It was exhibited, together with the version now in New York, in the Burlington Fine Arts Club in London in 1898 and in Edinburgh in 1992.

Since the painting was first discussed in depth by Möller (1926), art historians have regularly sought to attribute it directly to Leonardo or have assumed, as most recently in the case of Arasse (1998), that substantial parts of it were executed by the master himself. The areas of obvious weakness within the painting, such as the sky, the surface of the water and the landscape, have been put down to retouching by another hand. The pronounced distortions in the faces of the Virgin and Child nevertheless argue emphatically against an attribution to Leonardo. The broad cracks in Mary's cloak are also evidence of technical shortcomings, which one would not expect to find in panel paintings dating from Leonardo's artistic maturity. We must therefore assume that here, even more than in the New York version, only the original design can be attributed to Leonardo.

Literature: Möller, 1926; Vezzosi, 1982 and 1983; Béguin, 1983, p. 87; Bury, 1992; Gould, 1992; Pedretti, 1992; Kemp, 1992 and 1994; Arasse, 1998, pp. 325–327; Echinger-Maurach, 2000, pp. 133–136, 146–147; Starnazzi, 2000.

XXV Portrait of Lisa del Giocondo (Mona Lisa), 1503–1506 and later (1510?)
Oil on poplar, 77 x 53 cm
Paris, Musée du Louvre, Inv. 779

Apart from a crack to the left of centre, which is secured with a dovetail at the rear, the painting is in an excellent state of repair. The panel, which consists of a thin sheet of poplar, reveals fully intact borders around its periphery, which contradicts the notion, still current, that the painting was trimmed by several centimetres on its right and left-hand sides (Hours, 1954, p. 16; Ottino della Chiesa, 1967; Vecce, 1998, p. 422; Prater, 1999). The paint has been built up in a large number of thin layers in what must have been a lengthy process (Wolters, 1952). The subtle painterly execution is one of the finest in all of Leonardo's paintings. Transparent glazes containing a high proportion of binder combine to create extremely soft transitions, an effect that is heightened by the yellowish varnish. This varnish distorts the colour of the clothing and the sky, however, as emerges above all in the top quarter of the picture, where small areas of damage and sections that have not darkened with age reveal a fresher palette tending more to blue. A number of pentimenti can be seen on the fingers, where there may also have been some retouching.

The painting is probably identical with the portrait that Antonio de Beatis saw on 10 October 1517 (Beltrami, 1919, no. 238; Villata, 1999, no. 314) in Leonardo's workshop in Cloux (see below). It is subsequently named, along with a number of other paintings by Leonardo, in the 1525 inventory of Salaì's estate. Like the *Virgin and Child with St Anne*, therefore, it must have returned to Milan in 1519, immediately after Leonardo's death (Shell/Sironi, 1991; Villata, 1999, no. 333). The painting listed as forming part of Salaì's estate is mentioned again in a Milanese notarial document of 1531, where it is valued at a con-

siderably lower sum, however (Villata, 1999, no. 347). Why Leonardo's painting should have been mentioned again in 1531 has yet to be satisfactorily explained. The issue is further complicated by a document published only recently, which might be evidence that Salaì sold some pictures to a representative of the French king in 1518 (Jestaz, 1999). Although neither individual paintings nor the name of Leonardo are specified in the document, the enormous purchase price of the equivalent of 6250 *lire imperiali* suggests that Salaì was here selling his master's most important paintings (by way of comparison, the Leonardo paintings in Salaì's estate of 1525 [Shell/Sironi, 1991] were valued at just half this amount, while back in 1494, the agreed price for the *Virgin of the Rocks* was 800 *lire imperiali*). It is consequently possible that the *Mona Lisa* may have been acquired for François I as early as 1518 (the document published by Bertrand Jestaz in 1999 nevertheless needs further evaluation). Whatever the case, over the following years the portrait eventually reached Fontainebleau, something also confirmed by Vasari in his *Life of Leonardo*, which he had written by 1547. In *c.* 1542 the painting was on display in François I's *appartement des bains*, where it hung in the company of Leonardo's *Leda*, *Belle Ferronière* and *St John the Baptist* (Dimier, 1900, p. 281; Zöllner, 1997, p. 466). The *Mona Lisa* remained in the royal collection in Fontainebleau for the next two centuries. After Vasari (1550), it is mentioned by Cassiano del Pozzo (1625) and Père Dan (1642, p. 136), who also claimed that François I had bought the painting for 12 000 francs (Poggi, 1919, p. XXII). Towards the end of the 18th century, the portrait moved to Versailles and from there to the Tuileries in Paris, after which it returned to Versailles. Between 1800 and 1804 it hung in Napoleon's bedchamber, before finally passing to the Louvre (Ottino della Chiesa, 1967, p. 103; Zöllner, 1997). A stir was created on 21 August 1911 when the painting was stolen by Vincenzo Perugia, an Italian decorator (McMullen, 1976; Reit, 1981; Chastel, 1989). After Perugia had attempted to sell the portrait in Florence in the winter of 1913, it was recovered and then exhibited several times before being returned to France. Further exhibitions followed in Washington, DC, and New York in 1963 and in Tokyo and Moscow in 1974.

The most famous painting in the world was executed for the Florentine silk merchant Francesco del Giocondo (1460–1539), who commissioned the portrait of his wife, Lisa Gherardini (1479–after 1551?), probably to mark the birth of their second son, in December 1502, and the fact that they were moving into their own home in the spring of 1503 (Zöllner, 1993; 1994). We owe the first reference to the identity of the client and the approximate date of the commission – the period from 1500 – to Giorgio Vasari, who was certainly acquainted with members of the Giocondo family (Zöllner, 1993, 1995, p. 70) and may even have known Francesco or his wife Lisa. The commission for the portrait can be dated relatively precisely, too, from the fact that the young Raphael leaned closely upon Leonardo's *Mona Lisa* in the early female portraits (*Lady with the Unicorn*, Rome, Galleria Borghese, ill. p. 199, and a preliminary drawing for this portrait in the Louvre; *Maddalena Doni*,

Florence, Palazzo Pitti), which he executed in Florence between the end of 1504 and 1506 (Zöllner, 1994, pp. 20–24; Kress, 1999). These portraits by Raphael and earlier Florentine portraits of women undoubtedly confirm, moreover, that Leonardo's *Mona Lisa* forms part of a portraiture tradition that developed towards the end of the 15th century in Florence and found its consummate expression at Leonardo's hands after 1500 (cf. main text, p. 128). How much of the portrait of Lisa del Giocondo Leonardo completed before the end of his second Florentine period in 1506 remains a matter of debate. On the basis of Vasari's assertion that the portrait was still unfinished after four years, it can be assumed that Leonardo completed the painting at some point after 1506. - Although the precise date remains a matter of contention, over the last few years there has been a growing tendency to place the finished *Mona Lisa* amongst Leonardo's later works. Thus Carlo Pedretti (1957, pp. 133–141; 1973, and elsewhere), Martin Kemp (1981, pp. 263–270), Carlo Vecce (1998, pp. 324–326) and Pietro Marani (1989; 1999, pp. 187–207), for example, suggest that while the basic composition may have been formulated in *c.* 1503–1506, the portrait proper was completed much later, in 1513–1514 or 1516. This late dating is arrived at on stylistic grounds, with the design of the landscape, for example, being cited as evidence that the panel was completed after 1510. This argument is unconvincing, however, since desolate, alpine-style landscape backgrounds are also found in many of Leonardo's earlier paintings, such as the *Adoration* (Cat. V), the *Madonna with the Carnation* (Cat. III), the *St Jerome* (Cat. IX) and the *Virgin of the Rocks* (Cat. XI and XVI). In the New York version of the *Madonna of the Yarnwinder* (Cat. XXIII), which was probably executed under Leonardo's supervision by 1507 at the latest, this design principle reaches a provisional climax. If we date the *Madonna of the Yarnwinder* to before 1510 and assume that Leonardo exerted a direct influence upon its execution, it is hardly possible to view the landscape background in the *Mona Lisa* as a product of the years 1513 to 1516. We should also consider in this context the motif of the bridge, which appears in a very similar constellation in both the *Mona Lisa* and the New York version of the *Madonna of the Yarnwinder*. Bridges of this type – long, carried on arches and in the immediate vicinity of a barren rocky landscape – were unusual in Florentine paintings of this period (the bridges and landscapes in works by Baldovinetti and Botticini, for example, are quite different). The distinctly Leonardesque constellation of landscape and bridge found in the *Madonna of the Yarnwinder* thus speaks clearly against a late dating for the *Mona Lisa*. The portrait may thus possibly have been finished before 1510. Whatever the case, it remained in Leonardo's possession at least until 1518 (Jestaz, 1999) and possibly right up to his death (see above).

In view of the contradictory information provided by the early sources and of countless gaps in the surviving documentation, there have been no lack of attempts to query the identity of the sitter, given by Vasari as Lisa del Giocondo. The Anonimo Gaddiano introduced an element of confusion early on when he wrote of a portrait of Piero del Francesco del Giocondo. Piero was Lisa del Giocondo's eldest son, born in May 1496 and hence just seven years old

in *c.* 1503. It is most unlikely that Leonardo would have painted his picture; individual portraits of children were found primarily in court circles, not amongst the urban middle classes. More plausible is the suggestion that the Anonimo Gaddiano derived his information several years later from Piero del Giocondo, now an adult.

No less confusion was spread by Antonio de Beatis, who in October 1517 saw in Leonardo's workshop the portrait of a "certain Florentine lady", which he described in a letter as being for Giuliano de' Medici. Even though, in the same letter, Antonio de Beatis got Leonardo's age wrong and thought he was right-handed (Gould, 1975, pp. 110–111), we must take his statements seriously. It was probably indeed the *Mona Lisa* that he saw, but by now it would have been far too embarrassing to admit that the now famous Leonardo da Vinci, painter to the French king and previously active at the papal court in Rome, still kept in his workshop a picture that he had begun 14 years previously for an unknown Florentine merchant. For this reason, possibly, the portrait is instead described as a commission for the late Giuliano de' Medici, who had died one year earlier. Whatever the case, it is not possible to arrive, as Carlo Pedretti (1957) and more recently Carlo Vecce (1998, pp. 324–326, 334, 422) attempt to do, at a reliable identification of the portrait's sister on the basis of the account by de Beatis.

In view of the fact that the *Mona Lisa* falls into a specific genre of Florentine portraiture from the years between 1490 and 1508, alternative suggestions as to the identity of the young female sitter are rendered largely implausible. It has been frequently emphasized, moreover, that these suggestions rest on no solid foundations (Brown/Oberhuber, 1978, pp. 61–64; Shell/Sironi, 1991, pp. 98–99; Zöllner, 1993, pp. 115–116, 130–131). Only the suggestion that the sitter might be Isabella d'Este can claim a certain plausibility (Stites, 1970, pp. 329–337; Tanaka, 1976/1977; 1983, pp. 141–146, 286–287). Isabella d'Este's correspondence suggests, however, that despite her repeated requests, the Marchioness failed to persuade Leonardo to paint a portrait of her (Beltrami, 1919, nos. 103, 106–108, 110, 141, 142, 143, 152, 157, 173; Villata, 1999, nos. 144, 149–151, 154, 190, 191, 192, 200, 210, 227).

Amongst the various interpretations of the painting, the thesis that has attracted most support is that put forward by Donald Strong (1982), who sees in the *Mona Lisa* the symbolic triumph of Virtue over Time. Others view the background landscape in more concrete terms as a reflection of Leonardo's geological studies and as an illustration of his anthropomorphic world view (Perrig, 1980; Webster-Smith, 1985). It may be possible to interpret the water in the upper right-hand corner of the composition as a primeval sea, as it was described, for example, by Giovanni Villani (Kemp, 1981, p. 265). Lisa's smile is perhaps derived from literary conventions (Dante, Firenzuola; Kemp, p. 267; Arasse, 1999, p. 408) or from a type that Leonardo assimilated from Verrocchio's workshop (Gombrich, 1986). More recent interpretations attempt to understand the painting in terms of a specific Florentine portrait typology and the tastes and expectations of Florentine patrons. It can also be argued that Leonardo's use of *sfumato* enabled him to go beyond traditional conventions governing the portrayal of female virtue (Zöllner, 1993, 1994; Kress,

1995, 1999). The interpretations proposed in the 19th century, which on occasion view the *Mona Lisa* as a "femme fatale", are today of only historical interest (Boas, 1940; Turner, 1993).

Qualitatively good copies of the *Mona Lisa* are found in the Louvre in Paris, in the Prado in Madrid, in the Liverpool Art Gallery, in the Walters Art Gallery in Baltimore (Chastel, 1989), in the Hermitage in St Petersburg and in the Oslo Museum of Art. Further copies in smaller museums and in private collections deserve more detailed study, particularly since numerous copies were made between the 17th and the 19th centuries and in connection with the theft of the *Mona Lisa* in 1911 (Reit, 1981). Several copies (Zöllner, 1993, p. 133) and Leonardo's original painting feature painted pillars on either side of the sitter. In a number of variations (e.g. Baltimore, Liverpool, Oslo, Vernon Collection, New York; Earl of Wemyss Collection), as also in Raphael's *Lady with the Unicorn* (ill. p. 134) and its preparatory study, the pillars are considerably wider than in the original. Both the copies and the portraits by Raphael may therefore be derived from a cartoon by Leonardo showing broader pillars than the ones in the final painting. It is also possible, however, that the copyists widened the very narrow pillars in the original, or that wider pillars appeared on the *Mona Lisa*'s original frame, now lost. Examples of such frames are to be found in the 15th century (Dülberg, 1990, no. 168).

Not a copy in the true sense, but rather a variation upon the original, is the so-called *Monna Vanna*, a seated female figure whose upper body is naked. The best-known versions of the *Monna Vanna* are a cartoon in Chantilly and a painting in the Hermitage in St Petersburg. Starting from Antonio de Beatis's same reference to the portrait of a Florentine lady for Giuliano de' Medici (Beltrami, 1919, no. 238; Vecce, 1990, p. 56; Villata, 1999, no. 314), it has been repeatedly attempted to link the *Monna Vanna* in Chantilly with this portrait. Thus Arasse (1998, p. 466) takes up the hypothesis put forward by Brown (1978b), who proposes that the *Monna Vanna* represents the portrait of one of Giuliano de' Medici's mistresses, which Leonardo commenced in Rome between 1513 and 1516, but which he left unfinished. The cartoon in Chantilly, according to this hypothesis, goes back to this portrait. This argument is unconvincing, however, since de Beatis was probably referring to the *Mona Lisa*. The numerous variations upon this theme by French artists would sooner seem to suggest that the *Monna Vanna* arose only after Leonardo's death, as a derivation of the *Mona Lisa*. It is barely conceivable, moreover, that the anatomically unfortunate rendering of the *Monna Vana*'s nose, upper arm and lower arm could go back to a design by Leonardo, or that the master could have transformed the subtle angling of the *Mona Lisa*'s upper body into such an unhappy pose.

Literature: Vasari, 1550, p. 552; Vasari, 1568, IV, pp. 39–40; Vasari, 1965, pp. 266–267; Frey, 1892, p. 111 (Anonimo Gaddiano); Dimier, 1900, pp. 279–284; Poggi, 1919, pp. XXII–XXIII; Pedretti, 1957; McMullen, 1976; Brown/Oberhuber, 1978; Kemp, 1981, pp. 263–270; Reit, 1981; Strong, 1982; Béguin, 1983, pp. 74–76; Brejon de Lavergnée, 1987, no. 4; Chastel, 1989; Marani, 1989, no. 21; Shell/Sironi, 1991; Zöllner, 1993, 1994, 1997; Kress, 1995; Arasse, 1998, pp. 386–412; Kress, 1999.

XXVI Battle of Anghiari, Copy after Leonardo's wall-painting (Tavola Doria), 1504–1506
Oil on wood, 85 x 115 cm
Private Collection

Leonardo's most prestigious commission as a painter was his wall-painting of the *Battle of Anghiari* for the Sala Grande (Sala del Gran Consiglio) of the Palazzo Vecchio in Florence. This wall-painting, which the artist abandoned unfinished in the spring of 1506 having working on the project for less than three years and which was destroyed in the middle of the 16th century, portrayed a scene from the Battle of Anghiari of 1440, in which the Florentines won a victory over the Milanese troops near the small town of Anghiari. Leonardo probably painted his composition not on the west wall (Travers Newton/Spencer, 1982) but on the southern half of the east wall of the Sala Grande. Michelangelo's so-called *Battle of Casci-na* was to appear on the other half of the same wall. Assuming that the two paintings were indeed intended for the east wall, they would each have covered an area of some 7 x 17.5 metres (Micheli, 1971; Farago, 1994, p. 304; Bambach, 1999b, pp. 107–108).

The very extensive documentation (Isermeyer, 1964; Pedretti, 1968, pp. 58–78; Bambach, 1999, pp. 38, 292) relating to Leonardo's work on the *Battle of Anghiari* can be summarized as follows: in autumn 1503 the Florentine government, under the leadership of Piero Soderini, commissioned Leonardo to design and execute the wall-painting. The original contract for this commission, which is mentioned in a supplementary agreement of 4 May 1504 (see below), is believed lost. On 25 October Leonardo was given the key to the Sala del Papa in the monastery of Santa Maria Novella, where he was supposed to produce the cartoon for the painting (Villata, 1999, no. 183). The handing over of the key was followed by a number of payments, in December 1503 for renovations to the roof of the Sala del Papa (in Villata, 1999, no. 205, under December 1504), in January 1504 for

the supply of wood and in February 1504 for joinery and masonry work as well as for further deliveries of materials, which may relate to the erection of scaffolding in the Sala del Papa (Beltrami, 1919, nos. 132, 134, 136–137; Villata, 1999, nos. 187–188). The above-mentioned supplementary contract of 4 May 1504 (Beltrami, 1919, no. 140; Villata, 1999, no. 189) states that Leonardo has so far received 35 gold ducats. The artist is required by the same contract to complete the cartoon he has already begun at the latest by the end of February 1505, or alternatively to paint parts of the design on the wall (cf. main text, p. 136). Further payments for Leonardo's work as a painter were made in June 1504, together with payments for materials needed for the cartoon and possibly for the construction of scaffolding (Beltrami, 1919, nos. 145–146; Villata, 1999, no. 194). A delivery of painting materials is recorded on 30 August 1504, and documented a month later on 31 October is a payment instruction to the sum of 210 lire, corresponding to 30 gold ducats and relating to Leonardo's fee for the months of June and July (Beltrami, 1919, nos. 151, 153; Villata, 1999, nos. 199, 201). In December 1504 payments were issued for minor works in the Sala Grande and in February and March 1505 for a mobile scaffolding (Beltrami, 1919, nos. 154, 159–160; Villata, 1999, nos. 206, 211–212), something also mentioned by Vasari. Receipts that have survived for April, August and October 1505 relate primarily to materials for the scaffolding, for the substitute cartoon (see below) and for the actual painting (Beltrami, 1919, nos. 160, 165–166; Villata, 1999, nos. 218, 221–222). An indication of the progress of the commission is also provided by a note (Codex Madrid II, fol. 2r; Villata, 1999, no. 219) of 6 June 1505, in which Leonardo speaks of having started painting in the Grand Council Chamber. An analysis of Leonardo's purchases of cartoon paper from this same period confirms that he must have started work on the wall-painting at about this time: on 30 April 1505 the artist bought a substantial quantity of cartoon paper with which to

make a copy of his original cartoon. This substitute cartoon was the one used to transfer the composition onto the wall (Beltrami, 1919, no. 165; Villata, 1999, no. 218; Bambach, 1999b, pp. 116–127).

Leonardo then appears to have worked on the wall-painting without interruption until the spring of 1506. From a document of 30 May 1506, we learn that the artist has been granted a three-month leave of absence, on condition that he returns promptly at the end of this period (Beltrami, 1919, no. 176; Villata, 1999, no. 229). Leonardo failed to honour this commitment, however, and spent the next few years chiefly in Milan under the protection of the French king. The wall-painting remained unfinished, prompting the Florentine Signoria to complain bitterly on 9 October 1506 about their artist's breach of contract (Beltrami, 1919, no. 180; Villata, 1999, no. 236).

A dozen or so drawings by Leonardo's own hand and various contemporary copies give us an idea of what the original *Battle of Anghiari* must have looked like (*Leonardo & Venezia*, 1992, pp. 256–279; Piel, 1995; Zöllner, 1998, with a critical discussion of the relevant copies). The drawings reveal that the artist was thinking, in the early stages at least, of a broad composition incorporating several episodes from the battle. In both the original cartoon and the wall-painting itself, however, Leonardo reduced his composition to just one central group of mounted figures in combat, in other words to the decisive encounter in the battle, in which the Milanese on the left are on the point of losing their standard to the Florentine troops storming in from the right. The fact that Leonardo condensed his composition into the dramatically heightened portrayal of a single, decisive moment is evidenced by the copies based on the wall-painting itself (such as the so-called *Tavola Doria*, the copy in the Uffizi and a pen drawing from the Ruccellai Collection) and by drawings copied from the cartoon, which include the variation by Peter Paul Rubens in the Louvre (ill. pp. 138) and its derivatives (The Hague, Los Angeles). An up-to-date and detailed discussion of these copies can be found in Zöllner (1998). The most comprehensive overview of all the relevant visual and documentary material to be published to date is that by Friedrich Piel (1995), the value of whose contribution is compromised, however, by his unlikely hypothesis that the *Tavola Doria* (undoubtedly the best of the painted copies of the wall-painting) is an original by Leonardo and represents the "trial panel" mentioned in a description by the Anonimo Gaddiano (Frey, 1992, p. 114). In view of the tight deadline by which the wall-painting had to be completed, and Leonardo's protracted manner of working, it is unlikely that he would have executed a trial version of the *Battle of Anghiari*. The panel referred to by the Anonimo Gaddiano was probably one in which Leonardo was experimenting with technique – it was exposed to an open fire – and would certainly not have extended to a detailed figural composition.

As a starting-point from which to create his wall-painting, Leonardo was provided with details about the real-life Battle of Anghiari by his employers. In the Codex Atlanticus (74r–b and v–c/201; RLW § 669), we find an account of the battle written by Signoria secretary Agostino Vespucci, which goes back to Leonardo Dati's *Trophaeum Anglicum* of c. 1443

(PRC, I, pp. 381–382; Meller, 1985; Cecchi, 1996). Leonardo's final composition, however, was not in fact based on the information supplied by Vespucci, in which the capture of the Milanese standard is not mentioned. The battle for the standard is only described by two contemporary sources (Rubinstein, 1991, p. 281–283), namely the original Dati (Meller, 1985) and Neri di Gino Capponi, who writes in his *Commentarii* that the leader of the Florentine troops charged into battle with 400 riders in order "to attack and capture the enemy flag" (Capponi in Muratori, 1731, col. 1195). On the basis of historical sources (Flavio Biondo, Gino Capponi, Leonardo Dati, Niccolò Machiavelli etc.), it is possible to identify the battling horsemen with some certainty. The figures thus portray, from left to right, Francesco Piccinino and his father Niccolò, the commanders of the Milanese troops, and Piergiampaolo Orsini and Ludovico Scarampo (or Michelotto Attendolo?), two leaders of the allied papal and Florentine forces (Meller, 1985).

Efforts to reconstruct Leonardo's original intentions (e.g. by Pedretti, 1968; Gould, 1954; Farago, 1994) have also been joined by attempts to analyse the political iconography of the painting in the context of the overall decorative programme of the Sala Grande in the Palazzo Vecchio (Hartt, 1983; Rubinstein, 1991; Zöllner, 1998). Mention should also be made of the studies by Olle Cederlöf (1959/1961), who interpreted such iconographical details as the ram's head on Francesco Piccinino's chest and who pointed out the importance of *cassone* [marriage chest] painting for Leonardo's composition, an influence today attracting renewed attention (Polcri, 2002). Furthermore, it can be assumed that contemporaries would also have understood the two paintings by Leonardo and Michelangelo as an artistic battle between the two masters (dalli Regoli, 1994). The Anonimo Gaddiano and Vasari even suggest that an enmity existed between Leonardo and Michelangelo (Frey, 1892, p. 115; Vasari, 1568, IV, pp. 41–43), something that must have been born during this time. From Leonardo's biographers (Billi, Vasari) we can also deduce that Leonardo was using an experimental painting technique, one that would be responsible for the rapid deterioration of the paint surface.

Literature: Benedettucci, 1991, p. 103 (Billi); Frey, 1892, pp. 112, 114 (Anonimo Gaddiano); Vasari, 1550, pp. 552–553; Vasari, 1558, IV, pp. 41–43; Vasari, 1965, pp. 267–268; Lessing, 1935; Suter, 1937; Wilde, 1944; Pedretti, 1968; Kemp, 1981, pp. 234–247; Hartt, 1983; Held, 1985, pp. 85–88; Meller, 1985; Rubinstein, 1991; dalli Regoli, 1994; Piel, 1995; Cecchi, 1997; Zöllner, 1998; Bambach, 1999b; Polcri, 2002.

XXVII Virgin and Child with St Anne (St Anne and Mary with the infant Christ), c. 1502–1513 (?)
Oil on poplar, 168.5 x 130 cm
Paris, Musée du Louvre, Inv. 776 (319)

The support consists of four boards glued vertically together and reinforced at the rear with two softwood crosspieces. Two strips of oak with a combined width of 18 cm were added on, probably at some later date, to the two vertical sides of the panel. The picture thus originally, and at least until 1683 (as per an inventory of Charles Le Brun of 1683, in Brejon de Lavergnée, 1987, no. 390), measured only 112 cm wide. The painting, which remains unfinished in a number of places, is in only mediocre condition. Whether or not to embark on a restoration is currently the subject of heated debate (information kindly supplied by Cécile Scailliérez, June 2001). A vertical crack is clearly visible on the front and runs just to the left of centre from the top of the panel more or less to the Virgin's chest. The most finished elements of the composition are the heads of the figures and parts of the landscape. A varnish that has darkened with age covers the painting and takes away some of its brilliancy. While the figures are unanimously considered to be the work of Leonardo himself, some authors see the hand of an assistant in sections of the background (Goldscheider, 1960). Descriptions of the state of the painting vary (Wolters, 1952; Hours, 1954; Béguin, 1983).

The provenance of the painting is well documented. Antonio de Beatis mentioned seeing the painting during the visit he paid to Leonardo's workshop in Cloux in 1517 (Beltrami, 1919, no. 238; Villata, 1999, no. 314). There are two possibilities as to what happened to the painting in the years that followed. It may have been sold, along with a number of other paintings by Leonardo, to the king of France at the end of 1518; a document of 1518 speaks of a very high sum of money being paid to Leonardo's pupil Salaì, which possibly relates to a sale of paintings (Jestaz, 1999; Villata, 1999, no. 347; cf. Cat. XXV). Alternatively, following Leonardo's death it may have been taken back to Milan by Salaì, only to return shortly afterwards to France. A painting of St Anne certainly appears in the inventory of Salaì's estate drawn up in 1525 (Shell/Sironi, 1991, pp. 104–108; Villata, 1999, no. 313) and in another Milanese inventory of 1531 (Villata, 1999, no. 347). The first theory is supported by a passage from Paolo Giovio's short biography of Leonardo of c. 1523–1527: "There still survives a panel painting of the infant Jesus, who is playing with Mary his Mother and his grandmother Anne. The French king bought the painting and put it on display in his chapel" (Beltrami, 1919, no. 258; Villata, 1999, no. 337). Similar information – albeit possibly relating to a cartoon – is provided by Antonio Billi, who in 1527–1530 wrote of Leonardo: "He produced numerous wonderful drawings, including a Madonna with St Anne, which went to France" (Benedettucci, 1991, p. 103). This information was then repeated by the Anonimo Gaddiano (c. 1537–1547). Vasari subsequently amended the second edition of his *Lives of the Artists* (1568) to include the same reference to a cartoon of St Anne that had been taken to France. A Virgin and Child with St Anne and a lamb is lastly also described by Gerolamo Casio between 1525 and 1528, although no mention is made of the painting's location (Villata, 1999, no. 336). We owe another description of the painting to the humanist Janus Lascaris (1445–1535), who was in the employ of the French king between 1518 and 1534 (Goukowsky, 1957). Antonio da Trento, an artist documented in Fontainebleau from 1537 to 1540, also executed a woodcut after Leonardo's *Virgin and Child with St Anne* (Hind, 1949). Between c. 1518/19 and 1540 the picture is thus known to have been in France, although not in the *appartements des bains* in Fontainebleau with Leonardo's other paintings. After this, however, we lose track of the *Virgin and Child with St Anne* – until 1629, when it was supposedly purchased by Cardinal Richelieu in Casale Monferrato in Italy. In 1636 the Cardinal gave it to the king of France (Villot, 1849, no. 293; Poggi, 1919, p. XIX), and it subsequently appears in virtually all the inventories of the royal collections and the Louvre (Brejon de Lavergnée, 1987; Béguin, 1983).

The *Burlington House Cartoon*, which is dated to 1499–1501 and portrays St Anne, Mary, the infant Jesus and the infant John the Baptist (Cat. XX), is traditionally seen as the first of Leonardo's St Anne compositions. We know of a second version of the subject (without an infant St John, but with a lamb) from the description provided by Fra Pietro da Novellara in a letter of 3 April 1501 and from two more or less contemporary copies (Cat. XXIIa and b). Vasari (1568) describes what may be a third version including both a lamb and the infant St John. In the view of Johannes Nathan (1992), support for the existence of this third version is provided by a sketch of a *Kneeling Leda* of c. 1501 (RL 12337), on which the study for a St Anne composition can be made out underneath the Leda drawing. If we accept this interpretation, then the Louvre *Virgin and Child with St Anne* represents the fourth version of the subject. This fourth version must also date from Leonardo's second Florentine period of 1500–1506, since Raphael took up its pyramidal composition in several works from around 1507 (see below).

Three sheets containing altogether five preparatory studies by Leonardo have been linked with the *Virgin and Child with St Anne*. These are the sheets housed in London, Paris and Venice (Cat. 27–30), whereby the attribution of the verso of the London drawing is disputed and a question mark also hangs over the pen and ink sketch in Venice. To these may be added the sketch discovered by Nathan (1992) on the Windsor sheet RL 12337 beneath a drawing for a Leda composition. All of these studies relate to an early phase of the design process. The sketches in London and Paris, in particular, make it clear that the individual stages in the evolution of the final composition are mutually interconnected and are also closely related to the *Burlington House Cartoon* (Cat. XX), the Brescianino version (Cat. XXIIa) and the present painting in the Louvre. On the basis of Novellara's oft-cited letter of 3 April 1501, which provides us with the only really solid date, we may assume that Leonardo had by this point in time more or less arrived at the final design for his St Anne composition. In his subsequent drawings for the *Virgin and Child with St Anne*, Leonardo was simply concerned with details.

The controversy over the dating of the various versions of the *Virgin and Child with St Anne* has forced the discussion of its iconography into the background. Without knowing the specific context in which the commission arose, moreover, it is impossible to be categorical about its meaning. The fact that we do not know for whom the painting was executed or where it was destined to be hung means that its iconography can be interpreted in all sorts of different ways. Thus it has been connected, for example, with Louis XII's veneration of St Anne (Wasserman, 1971), with Maximilian I (Schapiro, 1956) and with the Florentine Republic, within which Leonardo may have been seeking to re-establish his position as an artist with a picture – executed on his own initiative – of St Anne, who was associated with Republican aspirations (Kemp, 1981, p. 226). For the present, however, we should confine ourselves primarily to generalized interpretations. Thus Pietro de Novellara (1501, Villata, 1999, no. 151) and Casio (c. 1525/28, Villata, 1999, no. 336) interpret the lamb as a symbol of the Passion and St Anne as the personification of the Church. The painting can also be viewed in conjunction with the revival in the cult of St Anne, which took place in the 1490s (Schapiro, 1956). It is also possible to interpret the landscape in the background as a reflection of Leonardo's "scientific" studies (Gantner, 1958, pp. 109–116, 137–160; Perrig, 1980; Fehrenbach, 1995, pp. 183–190) or in terms of religious symbolism (Battisti, 1991).

There is no disputing the extraordinary influence exerted by Leonardo's *Virgin and Child with St Anne*, whose pyramidal composition has become a defining feature of the High Renaissance. Before moving to Rome in 1508, Raphael drew on the painting (and/or its cartoon) in several of his works (e.g. the *Esterhazy Madonna* in Budapest, the *Madonna of the Goldfinch* in the Uffizi, *La Belle Jardinière* in the Louvre, the *Madonna of the Meadow* in Vienna and the *Canigiani Holy Family* in Munich). Over the next 20 years Leonardo's composition appears to have impacted first and foremost painting in Milan, since the majority of the surviving copies of the *Virgin and Child with St Anne* were executed by Lombard artists (see below). Some of these copies also contain echoes of the landscape of the Louvre version of the *Virgin and Child with St Anne*. The painting in its present form must therefore have been largely completed at some point between 1508 and 1513, the years corresponding to Leonardo's second and lengthier Milanese period. This suggestion is supported by the Kassel *Leda and her Children* (Cat. XXVIII), which arose in Milan c. 1508–1513 and which presupposes a detailed knowledge of the *Virgin and Child with St Anne*.

Qualitatively the best copies and variations upon the *Virgin and Child with St Anne* are found in the Uffizi in Florence (wood, 99 x 77 cm), the Wight Art Gallery of the University of California in Los Angeles (wood, 177.8 x 114.3 cm, formerly Leuchtenberg Collection, St Petersburg, from S. Maria presso S. Celso in Milan), the Strasburg University Gallery (oil on canvas, 187 x 127 cm, from S. Eustorgio in Milan), the Brera in Milan (wood, 158 x 108 cm) and the Prado in Madrid (105 x 74 cm). The Brera copy was probably based on a now lost cartoon of the *Virgin and Child with St Anne* (formerly in the Esterhazy Collection), whose provenance can be traced back to the collection of Padre Resta in the 17th century (Verga, 1931, no. 825; Poggi, 1919, p. XX). The variations in Los Angeles, Strasburg and the Prado all presuppose a knowledge of original drawings by Leonardo (Müller-Walde, V, 1899) or a lost cartoon. Good copies in which St Anne has been omitted hang in the Muzeum Narodowe in Poznan (oil on wood, 110 x 87 cm) and in the Museo Poldi-Pezzoli in Milan (Ottino della Chiesa, 1967, pp. 108–109; Marani, 1990, pp. 112, 146; Scailliérez, 2000, figs. 9, 11). The copies, which in many cases differ from the original painting in their palette and design of the draperies, deserve more detailed analysis.

Literature: de Beatis, 1517 (Beltrami, 1919, no. 238; Villata, 1999, no. 314); Salai's estate, 1525 (Shell/Sironi, 1991, pp. 104–108); Giovio, 1527 (Villata, 1999, no. 338); Benedettucci, 1991, p. 103 (Billi); Casio, 1528 (Villata, 1999, no. 336); Frey, 1892 (Anonimo Gaddiano), p. 112; Poggi, 1919, pp. XVI–XXII; Suida, 1929; Heydenreich, 1933; Wolters, 1952, pp. 136–137; Hours, 1954, pp. 19–20; Schapiro, 1956; Ottino della Chiesa, 1967, no. 35; Clark/ Pedretti, 1968, nos. 12526–12533; Béguin, 1983, pp. 77–79; Marani, 1987; Nathan, 1992; Bambach, 1999, pp. 250–251.

M. Davies, *National Gallery Catalogues. The Earlier Italian Schools*, London 1951
L. Dimier, *Le Primatice*, Paris 1900
C. Dionisotti, "Leonardo uomo di lettere", in: *Italia medioevale e umanistica*, 5, 1962, pp. 183–216
A. Dülberg, *Privatporträts. Geschichte und Ikonologie einer Gattung im 15. und 16. Jahrhundert*, Berlin 1990
C. Echinger-Maurach, "'Gli occhi fissi nella somma bellezza del Figliuolo'. Michelangelo im Wettstreit mit Leonardos Madonnenconcetti der zweiten Florentiner Periode", in: *Michelangelo. Neue Beiträge*, ed. M. Rohlmann and A. Thielemann, Munich/Berlin 2000, pp. 113–150
S.Y. Edgerton, Jr., *The Renaissance Rediscovery of Linear Perspective*, New York etc. 1975
K.R. Eissler, *Leonardo da Vinci. Psychonanalytic Notes on the Enigma*, New York 1961
J. Elkins, "The Case Against Surface Geometry", in: AH, 14, 1991, pp. 143–174
W.A. Emboden, *Leonardo da Vinci on Plants and Gardens*, Portland 1987
B. Fabjan/P.C. Marani (eds), *Leonardo. La dama con l'ermellino*, exh. cat., Rome 1998
A. Falchetti, *La Pinacoteca Ambrosiana*, Vicenza 1969 (2nd edn. 1986)
C.J. Farago, *Leonardo da Vinci's "Paragone": A Critical Interpretation With a New Edition of the Text in the Codex Urbinas*, Leiden etc. 1992
C.J. Farago, "Leonardo's Battle of Anghiari: A Study in the Exchange Between Theory and Practice", in: AB, 76, 1994, pp. 301–330
F. Fehrenbach, *Licht und Wasser. Zur Dynamik naturphilosophischer Leitbilder im Werk Leonardo da Vincis*, Tübingen 1997
F.M. Feldhaus, *Leonardo der Techniker und Erfinder*, Jena 1922
S. Ferino-Pagden, "From Cult Images to the Cult of Images. The Case of Raphael's Altarpieces", in: P. Humfrey/M.Kemp (eds.), *The Altarpiece in the Renaissance*, Cambridge 1990, pp. 165–189
S. Ferino-Pagden (ed.), *"La prima donna del mondo". Isabella d'Este. Fürstin und Mäzenatin der Renaissance*, exh. cat., Vienna 1994
G. Ferri Piccaluga, "La prima versione della Vergine delle Rocce", in: ALV, 7, 1994, pp. 43–50
M.T. Fiorio, *Giovanni Antonio Boltraffio. Un pittore milanese nel lume di Leonardo*, Milan/Rome 2000
J. Fletcher, "Bernardo Bembo and Leonardo's Portrait of Ginevra de'Benci", in: BM, 131, 1989, pp. 811–816
R. Fritz, "Zur Ikonographie von Leonardos Bacchus-Johannes", in: *Museion. Studien aus Kunst und Geschichte für Otto H. Förster*, Cologne 1960, pp. 98–101
L. Fusco/G. Corti, "Lorenzo de'Medici on the Sforza Monument", in: ALV, 5, 1992, pp. 11–32
P. Galluzzi, "The Career of a Technologist", in: *Leonardo. Engineer and Architect*, 1987, pp. 41–109
A. Gamberini/F. Somaini, *L'Età dei Visconti e degli Sforza: 1277–1535*, Milan 2001
C. Gandelmann, "Der Gestus des Zeigers", in: Kemp, 1992, pp. 71–93
J. Gantner, *Leonardos Visionen von der Sintflut und vom Untergang der Welt*, Berne 1958
E. Gibson, "Leonardo's Ginevra de'Benci. The Restauration of a Renaissance Masterpiece", in: *Apollo*, 133, 1991, pp. 161–165
C. Gilbert, "Last Suppers and their Refectories", in: *The Pursuit of Holiness in Late Medieval and Renaissance Religion*, ed. Charles Trinkaus and Heiko A. Obermann, Leyden 1974, pp. 371–407
Gilbert, see also 2.2. Sources
L. Giordano, "L'autolegittimazione di una dinastia: gli Sforza e la politica dell'immagine", in: *Artes*, 1, 1993, pp. 7–33
L. Giordano, *Ludovicus Dux: L'immagine del potere*, Vigevano 1995
H. Glasser, *Artists' Contracts of the Early Renaissance*, PhD thesis 1965, New York 1977
R. Goffen, *Icon and Vision: The Half-Length Madonna of Giovanni Bellini*, PhD thesis, New York 1974, Ann Arbor 1976
L. Goldscheider, *Leonardo da Vinci, Life and Work, Paintings and Drawings*, London 1959
E.H. Gombrich, "Leonardo's Grotesque Heads. Prolegomena to Their Study", in: *Leonardo. Saggi e ricerche*, 1954, pp. 199–219
E.H. Gombrich, "Leonardo's Method of Working out Compositions", in: Gombrich, *Norm and Form*, Oxford 1966, pp. 58–63
E.H. Gombrich, "Ideal and Type in Italian Renaissance Painting", in: Gombrich, *New Light on Old Masters*, Oxford 1986, pp. 89–124
M. Goukowsky, "Du nouveau sur Léonard de Vinci. Léonard et Janus Lascaris", in: *Bibliothèque d'humanisme et renaissance*, 19, 1957, pp. 7–13
C. Gould, "The Newly-Discovered Documents Concerning Leonardo's Virgin of the Rocks and their Bearing on the Problem of the Two Versions", in: AeH, 2, 1981, pp. 73–76
C. Gould, "La Vergine delle Rocce", in: *Leonardo. La pittura*, 1985, pp. 56–63
C. Gould, "Leonardo's Madonna of the Yarnwinder. Revelations of Reflectogram Photography", in: *Apollo*, 136, 1992, 365, pp. 12–16
C. Gould, "The Early History of Leonardo's Vierge aux Rochers", in: GBA, 124, 1994, pp. 216–222
G. Gronau, "Ein Jugendwerk des Leonardo da Vinci", in: *Zeitschrift für Bildende Kunst*, 23, 1912, pp. 253–259
S. Grossman, "The Madonna and Child with a Pomegranate and Some Paintings from the Circle of Verrocchio", in: *National Gallery of Art. Report and Studies in the History of Art*, [2], 1968, pp. 47–69
J. Guiffrey, "La Collection de M. Gustave Dreyfus II", in: *Les artes*, [17], 1908, fasc. 71, p. 2015
M.A. Gukovskij, *Madonna Litta* [in Russian], Moscow 1959
S. Hager (ed.), *Leonardo, Michelangelo, and Raphael in Renaissance Florence from 1500 to 1508*, Washington, DC, 1992
N. Hamilton, *Die Darstellung der Anbetung der heiligen drei Könige in der toskanischen Malerei von Giotto bis Lionardo*, Strasburg 1901
E. Harding/A. Braham et al., "The Restoration of the Leonardo Cartoon", in: *National Gallery Technical Bulletin*, 13, 1989, pp. 4–27
F. Hartt, "Leonardo and the Second Florentine Republic", in: *Journal of the Walters Art Gallery*, 44, 1983, pp. 95–116
R. Hatfield, "The Compagnia de'Magi", in: JWCI, 33, 1970, pp. 107–161
R. Hatfield, *Botticelli's Uffizi "Adoration". A Study in Pictorial Content*, Princeton 1976
G.W. F. Hegel, *Vorlesungen über die Philosophie der Geschichte* (Werke, XII), 4th edn., Frankfurt 1995
J.S. Held, Rubens. *Selected Drawings*, 2nd edn, Oxford 1986
[P. Hendy], *National Gallery Catalogues. Acquisitions 1953–1962*, London, undated [1963]
V. Herzner, *Jan van Eyck und der Genter Altar*, Worms 1995
L.H. Heydenreich, *Die Sakralbau-Studien Leonardo da Vinci's*, Leipzig 1929
L.H. Heydenreich, "La Sainte-Anne de Léonard de Vinci", in: GBA, 10, 1933, pp. 205–219
L.H. Heydenreich, "Vier Bauvorschläge Lionardo da Vincis an Sultan Bajezid II.", in: Heydenreich, 1988, pp. 53–60
L.H. Heydenreich, *Leonardo da Vinci*, 2 vols, Basle 1953
L.H. Heydenreich, "Bemerkungen zu den Entwürfen Leonardos für das Grabmal Gian Giacomo Trivulzios", in: Heydenreich, 1988, pp. 123–134
L.H. Heydenreich, *The Last Supper*, London 1974
L.H. Heydenreich, "La Madonna del Garofano", in: *Leonardo. La pittura*, 1985, pp. 29–45
L.H. Heydenreich, *Leonardo-Studien*, ed. G. Passavant, Munich 1988
R. Hiller von Gaertringen, "Drawing and Painting in the Italian Renaissance Workshop" [rev. by Bambach, 1999], in: *Apollo*, 153, 2001 (no. 3), pp. 53–54
P. Hills, "Leonardo and Flemish Painting", in: BM, 122, 1980, pp. 609–615
A.M. Hind, "A Chiaroscuro Woodcut after Leonardo da Vinci", in: BM, 91, 1949, pp. 164–165
Hochrenaissance im Vatikan. Kunst und Kultur im Rom der Päpste I, 1503–1534, exh. cat., Bonn 1998
B. Hochstetler Meyer, "Leonardo's Hypothetical Painting of Leda and the Swan", in: MKIF, 34, 1990, pp. 279–294
V. Hoffmann, "Leonardos Ausmalung der Sala delle Asse im Castello Sforzesco", in: MKIF, 16, 1972, pp. 51–62
W. Hood, *Fra Angelico at San Marco*, New Haven/London 1993
H. Horne, *The Life of Leonardo da Vinci by Giorgio Vasari*, London 1903
M. Hours, "Étude analytique des tableaux de Léonard de Vinci au Laboratoire du Musée du Louvre", in: *Leonardo. Saggi e ricerche*, 1954, pp. 13–25
C.A. Isermeyer, "Die Arbeiten Leonardos und Michelangelos für den grossen Ratssaal in Florence", in: *Studien zur Toskanischen Kunst. Festschrift for L.H. Heydenreich*, Munich 1964, pp. 83–130
B. Jestaz, "François Ier, Salaì et les tableaux de Léonard", in: *Revue de l'art*, 126, 1999, pp. 68–72
G. Kaftal, *Iconography of the Saints in Tuscan Painting*, Florence 1952
K.D. Keele, *Leonardo da Vinci's Elements of the Science of Man*, New York/London etc. 1983
H. Kehrer, *Die heiligen drei Könige in Literatur und Kunst*, 2 vols, Leipzig 1908–1909
L. Keith/A. Roy, "Giampietrino, Boltraffio, and the Influence of Leonardo", in: *National Gallery Technical Bulletin*, 17, 1996, pp. 4–19
M. Kemp, "'Il concetto dell'anima' in Leonardo's Early Skull Studies", in: JWCI, 34, 1971, pp. 115–134
M. Kemp, "Dissection and Divinity in Leonardo's Late Anatomies", in: JWCI, 35, 1972, pp. 200–225
M. Kemp, "'Ogni dipintore dipinge sé': A Neoplatonic Echo in Leonardo's Art Theory?", in: *Cultural Aspects of the Italian Renaissance. Essays in Honour of Paul Oskar Kristeller*, ed. C.H. Clough, New York 1976, pp. 311–323
M. Kemp/A. Smart, "Leonardo's Leda and the Belvedere River-Gods", in: AH, 3, 1980, pp. 182–193
M. Kemp, *Leonardo da Vinci. The Marvellous Works of Nature and Man*, London 1981
M. Kemp/J. Roberts (eds), *Leonardo da Vinci*, exh. cat., London 1989
M. Kemp, *The Science of Art. Optical Themes in Western Art from Brunelleschi to Seurat*, New Haven/London 1990
M. Kemp (ed.), *Leonardo da Vinci. The Mystery of the "Madonna of the Yarnwinder"*, Edinburgh 1992
M. Kemp, "From Scientific Examination to the Renaissance Art Market: The Case of Leonardo da Vinci's Madonna of the Yarnwinder", in: *Journal of Medieval and Renaissance Studies*, 24, 1994, pp. 259–274
M. Kemp, *Der Blick hinter die Bilder. Text und Kunst in der italienischen Renaissance*, Cologne 1997
W. Kemp (ed.)., *Der Betrachter ist im Bild. Kunstwissenschaft und Rezeptionsästhetik*, 2nd edn, Berlin 1992
D. Kiang, "Gasparo Visconti's Pasitea and the Sala delle Asse", in: ALV, 2, 1989, pp. 101–109
W. Köhler, "Michelangelos Schlachtkarton", in: *Kunstgeschichtliches Jahrbuch der kaiserlich-königlichen Zentralkommission*, 1, 1907, pp. 115–172
S. Kress, *Das autonome Porträt in Florence*, PhD thesis, Gießen 1995
S. Kress, "Memlings Triptychon des Benedetto Portinari und Leonardos Mona Lisa", in: C. Kruse/F. Thürlemann (eds), *Porträt – Landschaft – Interieur. Jan van Eycks Rolin-Madonna im ästhetischen Kontext*, Tübingen 1999, pp. 219–235
A. Kreul, *Leonardo da Vincis Hl. Johannes der Täufer. Sinnliche Gelehrsamkeit oder androgynes Ärgernis?* Osterholz-Scharmbeck 1992
E. Kris/O. Kurz, *Die Legende vom Künstler. Ein geschichtlicher Versuch*, Frankfurt/Main 1980
P.O. Kristeller, *Humanismus und Renaissance*, 2 vols, Munich 1976
H. Kühn, "Naturwissenschaftliche Untersuchung von Leonardos Abendmahl in Santa Maria delle Grazie in Milan", in: *Maltechnik Restauro*, 91 (4), 1985, pp. 24–51
R. Kultzen, *Alte Pinakothek München. Katalog V. Italienische Malerei*, Munich 1975
T.K. Kustodieva, *The Hermitage. Catalogue of Western European Painting. Italian Painting. Thirteenth to Sixteenth Centuries*, Florence 1994
M.W. Kwakkelstein, *Leonardo da Vinci as a Physiognomist. Theory and Drawing Practice*, Leiden 1994
K. Kwiatkowski, *"La Dame à l'Hermine" de Léonard de Vinci. Étude technologique*, Wroclaw 1955
L'Annunciazione di Leonardo. La montagna sul mare, ed. A. Natali, place of publication not given, 2000 [2001]
D. Laurenza, *"De figura umana". Fisiognomica, anatomia e arte in Leonardo*, Florence 2001
J.M. Lehmann, *Staatliche Kunstsammlungen Kassel. Gemäldegalerie Alte Meister, Schloss Wilhelmshöhe. Italienische, französische und spanische Gemälde des 16. bis 18. Jahrhunderts*, Fridingen 1908
I Leonardeschi ai raggi "X", ed. M.P. Garberi, Milan 1972
Leonardo e il mito di Leda, ed. G. dalli Regoli, R. Nanni and A. Natali, exh. cat., Vinci 2001
Leonardo e l'incisione. Stampe derivate da Leonardo e Bramante dal XV al XIX secolo, ed. C. Alberici, exh. cat., Milan 1984
Leonardo & Venezia, exh. cat., Milan 1992
Leonardo. La pittura, ed. M. Alpatov, D. Arasse et al., 2nd edn., Florence 1985
Leonardo. Saggi e ricerche, Rome 1954
M. Lessing, *Die Anghiari-Schlacht des Leonardo da Vinci. Vorschläge zur Rekonstruktion*, Quakenbrück 1935
F. Leverotti, "La crisi finanziaria del ducato di Milano alla fine del Quattrocento", in: *Milano nell'età di Lodovico il Moro. Atti del convegno internazionale 1983*, 2 vols, Milan 1983, II, pp. 585–632
M. Levi d'Ancona, "La Vergine delle Rocce di Leonardo: studio iconografico delle due versioni di Parigi e di Londra", in: AL, 1, 1955, pp. 98–104
M. Levi d'Ancona, *The Iconography of the Immaculate Conception in the Middle Ages and Early Renaissance*, place of publication not given, 1957
J. Liebrich, *Die Verkündigung an Maria. Die Ikonographie der italienischen Darstellungen von den Anfängen bis 1500*, Cologne 1997
R. Lightbown, *Mantegna*, Oxford 1986
M. Lisner, "Leonardos Anbetung der Könige. Zum Sinngehalt und zur Komposition", in: ZfKG, 44, 1981, pp. 201–242
Maestri e botteghe. Pittura a Firenze alla fine del Quattrocento, ed. M. Gregori et al., exh. cat., Florence/Milan 1992
F. Malaguzzi-Valeri, *La corte di Lodovico il Moro*, 4 vols, Milan 1915–1923
É. Mâle, "Les Rois mages et le drame liturgique", in: GBA, 4, 1910, pp. 261–270
P.C. Marani, *L'architettura fortificata negli studi di Leonardo da Vinci*, Florence 1984
P.C. Marani, *Leonardo e i leonardeschi a Brera*, Florence 1987
P.C. Marani, *Leonardo. Catalogo completo dei dipinti*, Florence 1989
P.C. Marani, *Leonardo e i leonardeschi nei musei della Lombardia*, Milan 1990
P.C. Marani, "Giovan Pietro Rizzoli detto il Giampietrino", in: *I Leonardeschi. L'eredità di Leonardo in Lombardia*, Milan 1998, pp. 275–300
P.C. Marani, *Leonardo. Una carriera di pittore*, Milan 1999
G. Martelli, "Il refettorio di Santa Maria delle Grazie in Milano e il restauro di Luca Beltrami nell'ultimo decennio dell'Ottocento", in: *Bollettino d'arte*, 65, 1980, pp. 55–72
I. Marzik, "Die Gestik in der *Storia* Leon Battista Albertis", in: Beyer/Prinz (ed), 1987, pp. 277–288
R. McMullen, *Mona Lisa. The Picture and the Myth*, London 1976
P. Meller, "La Battaglia d'Anghiari", in: *Leonardo. La pittura*, 1985, pp. 130–136
C. Merzenich, *Vom Schreinerwerk zum Gemälde. Florentiner Altarwerke der ersten Hälfte des Quattrocento*, Berlin 2001
J. Meyer/W. v. Bode, *Königliche Museen. Gemälde-Galerie. Beschreibendes Verzeichnis*, Berlin 1878
J. Meyer zur Capellen, *Raphael in Florence*, Munich/London 1996
P. Micheli, "Alla ricerca della prima sala", in: *Notiziario del Comune* [di Firenze], no. 3/4, 1971, pp. 20–22
K. Moczulska, "The Most Graceful and the Most Exquisite gallée in the Portrait of Leonardo da Vinci", in: *Folia historiae artium*, 1, 1995, pp. 55–76 (in Polish), 77–86 (in English)
E. Möller, "Leonardo's Madonna with the Yarnwinder", in: BM, 49, 1926, pp. 61–68
E. Möller, "Leonardos Madonna mit der Nelke in der Älteren Pinakothek", in: *Münchner Jahrbuch der bildenden Kunst*, 12, 1937, pp. 5–40
E. Möller, "Leonardos Bildnis der Ginevra dei Benci", in: *Münchener Jahrbuch der bildenden Kunst*, 12, 1937/1938, pp. 185–209
E. Möller, *Das Abendmahl des Lionardo da Vinci*, Baden-Baden 1952
B. Morley, "The Plant Illustrations of Leonardo da Vinci", in: BM, 121, 1979, pp. 553–560
P.L. Mulas, "'Cum aparatu ac triumpho quo pagina in hac licet aspicere'. L'investitura ducale di Ludovico Sforza, il messale Arcimboldi e alcuni problemi di miniatura Lombarda", in: *Artes*, 2, 1994, pp. 5–38
P. Müller-Walde, "Beiträge zur Kenntnis des Leonardo da Vinci", in: *Jahrbuch der Königlich Preussischen Kunstsammlungen*, 18, 1897, pp. 92–169 [I–II]; 19, 1898, pp. 225–266 [III–IV]; 20, 1899, pp. 54–116 [V–VII]
E.J. Mundy, "Porphyry and the Posthumous Fifteenth Century Portrait", in: *Pantheon*, 46, 1988, pp. 37–43
A. Nagel, "Leonardo and sfumato", in: *RES. anthropology and aesthetics*, 24, 1993, pp. 7–20
A. Natali, "Lo Sguardo degli angeli. Tragitto indiziario per il Battesimo di Cristo di Verrocchio e Leonardo", in: MKIF, 42, 1998, pp. 252–273

A. Natali, "Il tempio e la radice", in: E. Cropper (ed.), *Florentine Drawing at the Time of Lorenzo the Magnificent*, Bologna 1994, pp. 147–156
J. Nathan, "Some Drawing Practices of Leonardo da Vinci: New Light on the Saint Anne", in: MKIF, 36, 1992, pp. 85–102
J. Nelson, "The High Altarpiece of SS. Annunziata in Florence: History, Form, and Function", in: BM, 139, 1997, pp. 84–94
A. Nova, "Die Legende des Künstlers: Beuys und Leonardo", in: *Der Codex Leicester*, exh. cat. Munich/Berlin 1999, pp. 59–69
C.D. O'Malley/J.B. de C.M. Saunders, *Leonardo da Vinci on the Human Body*, New York 1952
H. Ost, *Leonardo-Studien*, Berlin/New York 1975
H. Ost, *Das Leonardo-Porträt in der Kgl. Bibliothek Turin und andere Fälschungen des Giuseppe Bossi*, Berlin 1980
A. Ottino della Chiesa, *Bernardino Luini*, Novara 1956
W. and E. Paatz, *Die Kirchen von Florenz*, 6 vols, Frankfurt/Main 1940–1954
E. Panofsky, *Studies in Iconology. Humanistic Themes in the Art of the Renaissance*, New York 1962
G. Passavant, *Andrea del Verrocchio als Maler*, Düsseldorf 1959
G. Passavant, *Verrocchio. Sculptures, Paintings and Drawings*, London 1969
C. Pedretti, *Studi vinciani*, Geneva 1957
C. Pedretti, *Leonardo da Vinci. Fragments at Windsor Castle from the Codex Atlanticus*, London 1957 (Pedretti, 1957a)
C. Pedretti, "A Ghost Leda", in: RV, 20, 1964, pp. 379–383
C. Pedretti, "A Sonnet by Giovan Paolo Lomazzo on the Leda of Leonardo", in: RV, 20, 1964, pp. 374–378
C. Pedretti, *Leonardo da Vinci inedito. Tre saggi*, Florence 1968
C. Pedretti, "The Burlington House Cartoon", in: BM, 110, 1968, pp. 22–28
C. Pedretti, *Leonardo da Vinci. The Royal Palace at Romorantin*, Cambridge (Mass.) 1972
C. Pedretti, *Leonardo. A Study in Chronology and Style*, New York/London 1973
C. Pedretti, *The Literary Works of Leonardo da Vinci. Commentary*, 2 vols, Oxford 1977
C. Pedretti, *Leonardo da Vinci Architekt*, Stuttgart/Zurich 1980
C. Pedretti, "Leonardo dopo Milano", in: Vezzosi, 1983, pp. 43–59
C. Pedretti, *Studies for the Last Supper from the Royal Library at Windsor Castle*, Washington, DC, 1983 (Pedretti, 1983a)
C. Pedretti, "Leonardo at the Städel Museum", in: ALV, 2, 1989, pp. 166–167
C. Pedretti, "La dama dell'ermellino come allegoria politica", in: *Studi politici in onore di Luigi Firpo*, ed. S. Rota Ghibaudi et al., I, Milan 1990, pp. 161–181
C. Pedretti, "Mirator veterum", in: ALV, 4, 1991, pp. 253–255
C. Pedretti, "The Mysteries of a Leonardo Madonna, mostly Unsolved", in: ALV, 5, 1992, pp. 169–175
C. Pedretti, "Leonardo in Sweden", in: ALV, 6, 1993, pp. 200–211
A. Perrig, "Leonardo: Die Anatomie der Erde", in: *Jahrbuch der Hamburger Kunstsammlungen*, 25, 1980, pp. 51–80
F. Piel, *Tavola Doria: Leonardo da Vincis modello zu seinem Wandgemälde der "Anghiarischlacht"*, Munich 1995
A. Pizzorusso, "Leonardo's Geology: A Key to Identifying the Works of Boltraffio, D'Oggiono and Other Artists", in: RV, 27, 1997, pp. 357–371
F. Polcri (ed.), *Una Battaglia nel Mito*, Florence 2002
J. Polzer, "The Perspective of Leonardo Considered as a Painter", in: M. Dalai Emiliani (ed.), *La prospettiva rinascimentale. Codificazioni e trasgressioni*, Florence 1980, pp. 233–247
J. Pope-Hennessy, *The Portrait in the Renaissance*, Princeton 1966
A.E. Popham, *The Drawings of Leonardo da Vinci With a New Introductory Essay by M. Kemp*, London 1994
A.E. Popham/P. Pouncey, *Italian Drawings in the Department of Prints and Drawings in the British Museum, The Fourteenth and Fifteenth Centuries*, 2 vols, London 1950
H. Posse, *Königliche Museen zu Berlin. Die Gemäldegalerie des Kaiser-Friedrich-Museums. Vollständiger beschreibender Katalog. Erste Abteilung. Die Romanischen Länder*, Berlin 1909
A. Prater, "Sehnsucht nach dem Chaos. Versuch über das Sfumato der Mona Lisa", in: *Ikonologie und Didaktik. Begegnungen zwischen Kunstwissenschaft und Kunstpädagogik*, ed. J. Kirschenmann et al., Weimar 1999, pp. 89–105
Raffaello a Firenze, exh. cat., Florence 1984
G. dalli Regoli, *Mito e scienza nella "Leda" di Leonardo* (XXX Lettura Vinciana), Florence 1991
G. dalli Regoli, "Leonardo e Michelangelo: il tema della Battaglia agli inizi del Cinquecento", in: ALV, 7, 1994, pp. 98–106
S.V. Reit, *The Day They Stole the Mona Lisa*, New York 1981
Renaissance Engineers from Brunelleschi to Leonardo da Vinci, exh. cat., ed. P. Galluzzi, Florence 1996
E.F. Rice, *Saint Jerome in the Renaissance*, Baltimore/London 1985
I.A. Richter, *Paragone. A Comparison of the Arts by Leonardo da Vinci*, London 1949
D. Rigaux, *A la table du Seigneur. L'Eucharistie chez les primitifs italiens (1250–1497)*, Paris 1989
D. Robertson, "'In Foraminibus Petrae': A Note on Leonardo's Virgin of the Rocks", in: *Renaissance News*, 7, 1954, pp. 92–95
M. Rossi/A. Rovetta, *Il Cenacolo di Leonardo. Cultura domenicana, iconografia eucaristica e tradizione lombarda*, Milan 1988
M. Rossi/A. Rovetta, *La Pinacoteca Ambrosiana*, Milan 1997
P. Rubin, "Commission and Design in Central Italian Altarpieces c. 1450–1550", in: E. Borsook/F. Superbi Gioffredi (eds), *Italian Altarpieces 1250–1550. Function and Design*, Oxford 1994, pp. 201–230
N. Rubinstein, "Machiavelli and the Mural Decoration of the Hall of the Great Council of Florence", in: *Musagetes*. Ed. R. Kecks, Berlin 1991, pp. 275–285
J. Ruda, *Fra Filippo Lippi. Life and Work with a Complete Catalogue*, London 1993
J. Rudel, "Bacco e San Giovanni Battista", in: *Leonardo. La pittura*, 1985, pp. 121–128
M. Rzepinska, "Light and Shadow in the Late Writings of Leonardo da Vinci", in: RV, 19, 1962, pp. 259–266
A. Salzer, *Die Beinamen Mariens in der deutschen Literatur und der lateinischen Hymnenpoesie des Mittelalters*, Linz 1893
C. Scailliérez, "La Vierge à l'Enfant avec sainte Anne de Léonard de Vinci: questions et hypothèses", in: *Au Louvre avec Viviane Forester*, Paris 2000, pp. 31–55
M. Schapiro, "Leonardo and Freud: An Art-Historical Study", in: *Journal of the History of Ideas*, 17, 1956, pp. 147–178
A. Scharf, *Filippino Lippi*, Vienna 1935
R. Schofield, "Amadeo, Bramante and Leonardo and the 'tiburio' of Milan Cathedral", in: ALV, 2, 1989, pp. 68–100
R. Schofield, "Leonardo's Milanese Architecture: Career, Sources and Graphic Techniques", in: ALV, 4, 1991, pp. 111–157
A. Schug, "Zur Ikonographie von Leonardos Londoner Karton", in: *Pantheon*, 26, 1968, pp. 446–455, and ibid., 27, 1969, pp. 24–35
D. Sedini, *Marco d'Oggiono. Tradizione e rinnovamento in Lombardia fra Quattrocento e Cinquecento*, Milan 1989
W. v. Seidlitz, *Leonardo da Vinci. Der Wendepunkt der Renaissance*, 2 vols, Berlin 1909
M. Sérullaz (ed.), *Le XVIe Siècle Européen. Dessins du Louvre*, Paris 1965
Lo sguardo degli angeli. Verrocchio, Leonardo e il "Battesimo di Christo", ed. A. Natali, place of publication not given, 1998
F.R. Shapley, *Catalogue of the Italian Paintings*. National Gallery of Art, Washington, DC, 1979
J. Shearman, "Leonardo's Colour and Chiaroscuro", in: ZfKG, 25, 1962, pp. 13–47
J. Shearman, *Only Connect ... Art and the Spectator in the Italian Renaissance*, Princeton 1992
J. Shell/G. Sironi, "Cecilia Gallerani: Leonardo's Lady with an Ermine", in: AeH, 13, 1992, pp. 47–66
J. Shell/G. Sironi, "Salaì and Leonardo's Legacy", in: BM, 133, 1991, pp. 95–108
J. Shell/G. Sironi, "Un nuovo documento di pagamento per la Vergine delle Rocce di Leonardo", in: *"Hostinato rigore". Leonardiana in memoria di Augusto Marinoni*, ed. P.C. Marani, Milan 2000, pp. 27–31
W. Smith, "Observations on the Mona Lisa Landscape", in: AB, 67, 1985, pp. 183–199
C.H. Smyth, "Venice and the Emergence of the High Renaissance in Florence: Observations and Questions", in: C. Bertelli (ed.) et al., *Florence and Venice: Comparisons and Relations*, Florence 1979, pp. 209–249
J. Snow Smith, *The Salvator Mundi of Leonardo da Vinci*, Seattle 1982
J. Snow Smith, "An Iconographic Interpretation of Leonardo's Virgin of the Rocks (Louvre)", in: AL, 67, 1983, pp. 134–142
J. Snow Smith, "Leonardo's Virgin of the Rocks (Musée du Louvre): A Franciscan Interpretation", in: *Studies in Iconography*, 11, 1987, pp. 35–94
H. von Sonnenburg, *Raphael in der Alten Pinakothek*, Munich 1983
C. Starnazzi (ed.), *La "Madonna dei Fusi" di Leonardo da Vinci e il paesaggio del Valdarno Superiore*, exh. cat., Arezzo 2000
R. Stefaniak, "On Looking into the Abyss: Leonardo's Virgin of the Rocks", in: *Konsthistorisk tidskrift*, 66, 1997, pp. 1–36
L. Steinberg, "Leonardo's Last Supper", in: *Art Quarterly*, 36, 1973, pp. 297–410
K.T. Steinitz, *Leonardo architetto teatrale e organizzatore di feste* (IX Lettura Vinciana), Florence 1970
C. Sterling, "Fighting Animals in the Adoration of the Magi", in: *Bulletin of the Cleveland Museum of Art*, 61, 1974, pp. 350–359
C. Sterling, *The Master of Claude, Queen of France*, New York 1975
R.S. Stites, *The Sublimations of Leonardo da Vinci*, Washington, 1970
V.I. Stoichita, *Eine kurze Geschichte des Schattens*, Munich 1999
D. Strong, "The Triumph of Mona Lisa: Science and Allegory of Time", in: *Leonardo e l'età della ragione*, 1982, pp. 255–278
W. Suida, "Leonardo's Activity as a Painter", in: *Leonardo. Saggi e ricerche*, pp. 315–329
W. Suida, *Leonardo und sein Kreis*, Munich 1929
D. Summers, "'Maniera' and Movement: The 'Figura Serpentinata'", in: *Art Quarterly*, 35, 1972, pp. 269–301
K.F. Suter, *Das Rätsel von Leonardos Schlachtenbild*, Strasbourg 1937
H. Tanaka, "Leonardo's Isabella d'Este. A New Analysis of the Mona Lisa in the Louvre", in: *Istituto Giapponese di Cultura in Roma. Annuario*, 13, 1976–1977, pp. 23–35
P. Tinagli, *Women in Italian Renaissance Art. Gender, Representation, Identity*, Manchester 1997
C. de Tolnay, "Remarques sur La Joconde", in: *La Revue des Arts*, 2, 1952, pp. 18–26
C. de Tolnay, *Michelangelo I. The Youth of Michelangelo*, Princeton 1969
P. Tonini, *Il santuario della Santissima Annunziata di Firenze*, Florence 1876
H. Travers Newton/J.R. Spencer, "On the Location of Leonardo's Battle of Anghiari", in: AB, 64, 1982, pp. 45–52
R.C. Trexler, *The Journey of the Magi. Meanings in the History of a Christian Story*, Princeton 1997
R.A. Turner, *Inventing Leonardo*, Berkeley/Los Angeles 1992
C. Vecce, *Leonardo*, Rome 1998
P.L. de Vecchi, "Iconografia e devozione dell'Immacolata in Lombardia", in: *Zenale e Leonardo*, 1982, pp. 254–257
J. Vegh, "Mediatrix omnium gratiarum. A Proposal for the Interpretation of Leonardo's Virgin of the Rocks", in: *Arte cristiana*, 80, 1992, pp. 275–286
K.H. Veltman, *Studies on Leonardo da Vinci I. Linear Perspective and the Visual Dimensions of Science and Art*, Munich 1986
P. Venturoli, "L'ancona dell'immacolata concezione di San Francesco Grande a Milano", in: *Giovanni Antonio Amadeo*, ed. J. Shell and L. Castelfranchi, Milan 1993, pp. 421–437
E. Verga, *Bibliografia vinciana 1493–1930*, 2 vols, Bologna 1931
A. Vezzosi (ed.), *Leonardo dopo Milano. La madonna dei fusi (1501)*, Florence 1982.
A. Vezzosi (ed.), *Leonardo e il leonardismo a Napoli e a Roma*, Florence 1983
F. Viatte, *Léonard de Vinci. Isabelle d'Este*, Paris 1999
E. Villata, "Il San Giovanni Battista di Leonardo: un'ipotesi per al cronologia e la committenza", in: RV, 27, 1997, pp. 187–236
E. Villata, "Ancora sul San Giovanni Battista di Leonardo", in: RV, 28, 1999, pp. 123–158
F. Villot, *Notice des tableaux exposés dans les galeries du Louvre*, 1st series, Paris 1849
M. Wackernagel, *The World of the Florentine Renaissance Artist. Projects and Patrons, Workshop and Art Market*, Princeton 1981
J. Walker, "Ginevra de' Benci by Leonardo da Vinci", in: *National Gallery of Art. Report and Studies in the History of Art 1967*, [2], 1968, pp. 1–38
M. Warnke, *Hofkünstler. Zur Vorgeschichte des modernen Künstlers*, Cologne 1985
J. Wasserman, "Michelangelo's Virgin and Child with Saint Anne at Oxford", in: BM, 111, 1969, pp. 122–131
J. Wasserman, "A Re-discovered Cartoon by Leonardo da Vinci", in: BM, 112, 1970, pp. 194–204
J. Wasserman, "The Dating and Patronage of Leonardo's Burlington House Cartoon", in: AB, 53, 1971, pp. 312–325
J. Wasserman, "Reflections on the Last Supper of Leonardo da Vinci", in: AL, 66, 1983, pp. 15–34
J. Wasserman, *Leonardo da Vinci*, New York 1984
W.J. Wegener, *Mortuary Chapels of Renaissance Condottieri*, PhD thesis, Princeton 1989
K. Weil Garris Posner, *Leonardo and Central Italian Art: 1515–1550*, New York 1974
E.S. Welch, *Art and Authority in Renaissance Milan*, New Haven/London 1995
M. Wiemers, *Bildform und Werkgenese. Studien zur zeichnerischen Bildvorbereitung in der italienischen Malerei zwischen 1450 und 1490*, Munich/Berlin 1996
J. Wilde, "The Hall of the Great Council of Florence", in: *Journal of the Warburg and Courtauld Institutes*, 7, 1944, pp. 65–81
R. and M. Wittkower, *Künstler – Aussenseiter der Gesellschaft*, Stuttgart 1989
H. Wohl, *The Paintings of Domenico Veneziano c. 1410–1461*, Oxford 1980
C. Wolters, "Über den Erhaltungszustand der Leonardobilder des Louvre", in: *Kunstchronik*, 5, 1952, pp. 135–144
J. Woods-Marsden, "Portrait of a Lady, 1430–1520", in: Brown, 2001, pp. 63–87
C. Yriarte, "Les Relations d'Isabelle d'Este avec Léonard de Vinci", in: GBA, 37, 1888, pp. 118–131
F. Zöllner, *Vitruvs Proportionsfigur*, Worms 1987
F. Zöllner, "Rubens Reworks Leonardo: The Fight for the Standard", in: ALV, 4, 1991, pp. 177–190
F. Zöllner, "'Ogni pittore dipinge sé'. Leonardo on 'automimesis'", in: *Der Künstler über sich in seinem Werk*, ed. M. Winner, Weinheim 1992, pp. 137–160
F. Zöllner, "Leonardo's Portrait of Mona Lisa del Giocondo", in: GBA, 121, 1993, pp. 115–138
F. Zöllner, *Leonardo da Vinci. Mona Lisa. Das Porträt der Lisa del Giocondo. Legende und Geschichte*, Frankfurt/Main 1994
F. Zöllner, "Karrieremuster: Das malerische Werk Leonardo da Vincis im Kontext der Auftragsbedingungen", in: *Georges-Bloch-Jahrbuch*, 2, 1995, pp. 57–73
F. Zöllner, "John F. Kennedy and Leonardo's Mona Lisa: Art as the Continuation of Politics", in: W. Kersten (ed.), *Radical Art History*, Zurich 1997, pp. 466–479
F. Zöllner, *La "Battaglia di Anghiari" di Leonardo da Vinci fra mitolgia e politica (XXXVII Lettura Vinciana)*, Florence 1998
F. Zöllner, "Leonardo da Vinci: Die Geburt der 'Wissenschaft' aus dem Geiste der Kunst", in: *Leonardo da Vinci. Der Codex Leicester*, exh. cat., Munich/Berlin 1999
V.P. Zubov, *Leonardo da Vinci*, Cambridge (Mass.) 1968

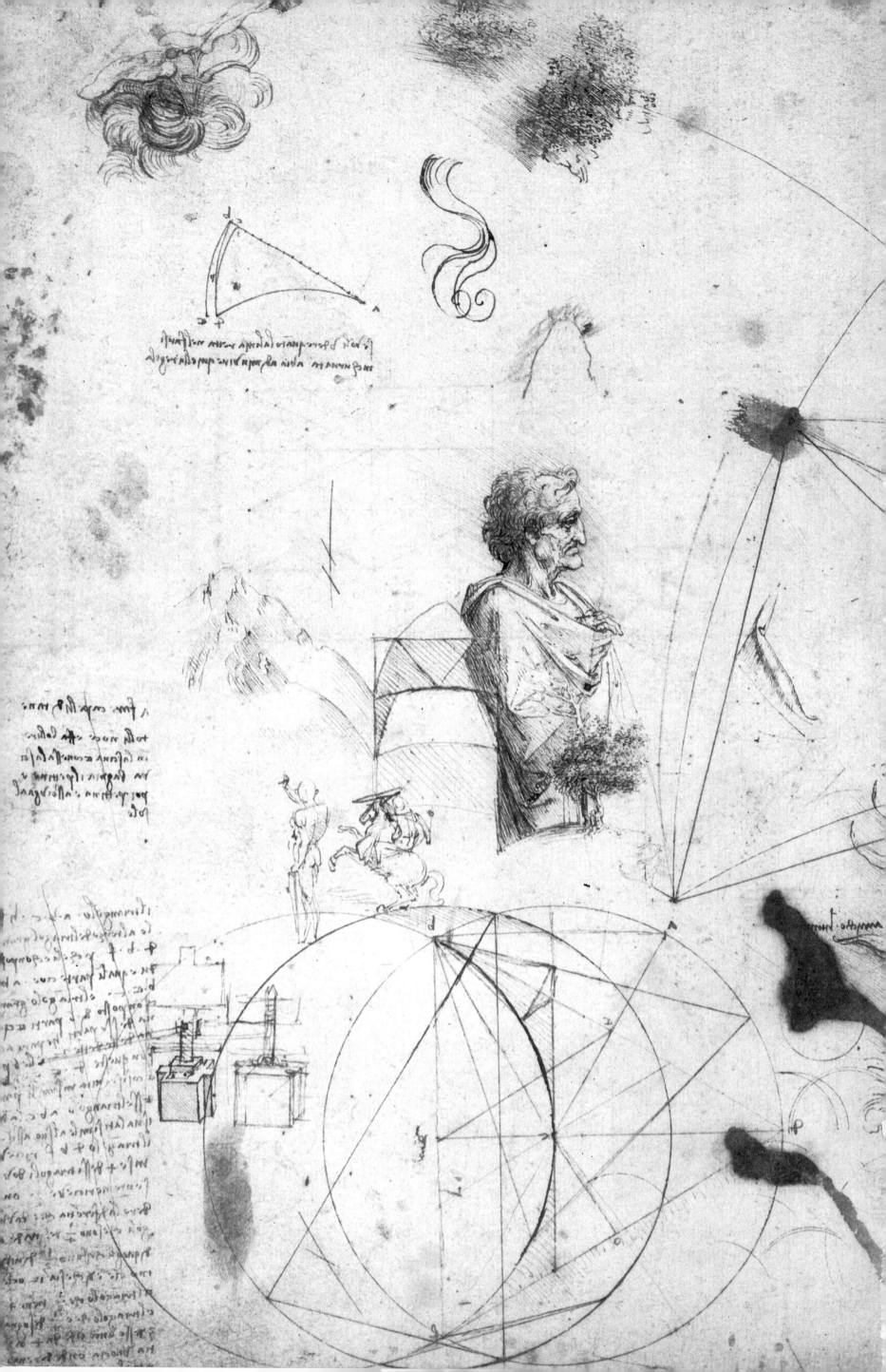